Fr. Titus Kieninger, ORC

THE ANGELS IN THE DIARY OF SAINT FAUSTINA KOWALSKA

Order of the Holy Cross, Inc.
Carrollton, OH
2014

Imprimi potest
P. Joachim Welz,
Prior General,
Rome, November 30, 2013

Imprimatur
Ecclesiastical approval granted by the Most Reverend Allen H. Vigneron, Archbishop of Detroit, 19 August 2014.

Quotations from the Diary of St. Maria Faustina Kowalska: Divine Mercy in My Soul - © 1987 Marian Fathers of the Immaculate Conception of the B.V.M. All rights reserved. Used with permission.

Divine Mercy (Blue Hyla) © Marian Fathers of the Immaculate Conception of the B.V.M.

St. Faustina and Divine Mercy Image © Marian Fathers of the Immaculate Conception of the B.V.M.

ISBN 9781942174004

No part of this publication may be reproduced, stored or transmitted in any form without the prior written permission.

Available from
Canons Regular of the Holy Cross
164 Apollo Road SE
Carrollton, OH 44615   1-330-738-3333

or

Work of the Holy Angels
opusangelorum.org

CONTENTS

0. Introduction... 7
   0.1 The faith of the Church 7
   0.2 The presence of the Angels in the life of Faustina Kowalska before entering the Convent 11
      0.2.1 At home with her family 11
      0.2.2 Member of the Religious Institute 12
   0.3 The Angelology in the Diary of Saint Faustina 13
1. The presence of the Angels in the Life of Saint Faustina 19
   1.1 The Guardian Angel 19
   1.2 The Consecration of Faustina and the Angels 25
   1.3 The Angels and their companionship, intercession and protection 26
2. The Angels and the Divine Mercy 31
   2.1 The divine action is marked by Mercy 31
      2.1.1 All was created by Divine Mercy 31
      2.1.2 The Divine Mercy - incomprehensible for men and Angels 33
   2.2 The "participation" of the Angels in God's perfections 35
   2.3 The fall of Angels 40
3. The faithful Angels: Who they are and how they manifest themselves 47
   3.1 The identity of Angels.. 47
      3.1.1 The different names for the Angels 47
         3.1.1.1 General names 47
         3.1.1.2 Particular names 48
      3.1.2 The Hierarchy of the Angels 51
      3.1.3 Groups of Angels 55
      3.1.4 Individual Angels 56
   3.2 The manifestations of the Angels to Saint Faustina 60
4. The preference of God for men 64
   4.1 God's Mercy and the Incarnation 65

- 4.1.1 The redeeming Incarnation 65
- 4.1.2 "The Angels were amazed" 68
- 4.2 The intimacy of God with men through the Eucharist 71
- 4.3 Consecration of human life to Christ 75
- 4.4 An exclusive secret 82
- 4.5 The Angels in zealous closeness and respectful distance 92
  - 4.5.1 The desired union with the Angels 93
  - 4.5.2 The angelic respectful distance 95
- 5. The Help of the Angels 102
  - 5.1 Help of higher Angels 102
    - 5.1.1 In spiritual Life 102
    - 5.1.2 In daily Life 106
  - 5.2 The Guardian Angel 109
    - 5.2.1 Three exceptional trips 109
    - 5.2.2 A special mission and "mysterious union" . 111
    - 5.2.3 Company, protection and consolation 113
- 6. The enemy of the sons of God 116
  - 6.1 The fact of diabolic attacks and their meaning ... 116
    - 6.1.1 The fact 116
    - 6.1.2 The universal fact 117
    - 6.1.3 The meaning of Faustina's experience 119
  - 6.2 Whom does the devil attack? where? and when? . 125
    - 6.2.1. Whom does the devil attack? 125
    - 6.2.2 Where does the devil attack? 126
    - 6.2.3. When does the devil attack? 127
  - 6.3 How does the devil attack? 129
    - 6.3.1 Sensible Attacks 129
    - 6.3.2 Touching the emotions 134
    - 6.3.3 "A multitude of thoughts" 137
  - 6.4 How can man defend himself against the attacks of the fallen angels? 143
    - 6.4.1 He seeks "lazy and idle souls" 144
    - 6.4.2 Silence 146
    - 6.4.3 "The Almighty is with her!" 149
    - 6.4.4 The holy Angels 152
    - 6.4.5 Profession of faith 156
    - 6.4.6 Prayer, sacraments, and sacramentals 157

6.4.6.1 Prayers	158
6.4.6.2 Sign of the Cross	159
6.4.6.3 Divine Mercy Chaplet	161
6.4.6.4 Sacraments	161
6.4.6.5 Holy Water	163
6.4.6.6 Sufferings and Prayers	164
6.4.7 Obedience	164
6.4.8 Active vigilance	168
Conclusion	172
The Angelology in the Diary of Saint Faustina	172

THE ANGELS IN THE DIARY OF SAINT FAUSTINA KOWALSKA

0. INTRODUCTION
0.1 THE FAITH OF THE CHURCH

Pope Benedict XVI spoke on many occasions about the holy Angels. He told the candidates for episcopacy at their ordination to shape their lives according the example of the three Archangels.[1] Saint John Paul II offered with his Catechesis from July 9th to August 20th, 1986 the most extensive doctrinal teaching of the *Magisterium* on the Angels. From this teaching, we learn that "the whole life of the Church benefits from the mysterious and powerful help of Angels (cf. *Acts* 5:18-20; 8:26-29; 10:3-8; 12:6-11; 27:23-25)"[2]. Additionally, we learn that:

> Angels have been present since creation and throughout the history of salvation, announcing this salvation from afar or near and serving the accomplishment of the divine plan: they closed the earthly paradise; protected ...; saved ...; communicated ...; led ...; announced ...; assisted ... (CCC 332).

---

[1] "From the Angel's task it is possible to understand the Bishop's service" (Homily on September 29, 2007).
[2] *Catechism of the Catholic Church* (= CCC), *Libreria Editrice Vaticana, 1997, 334.*

On the feast of the holy Archangels in 2008, the Holy Father Benedict XVI said:

> I said just now that (...) liturgy invites us to remember the holy Archangels, Michael, Gabriel and Raphael. Each one of them, as we read in the Bible, carried out a special mission in the history of salvation.
>
> Dear brothers and sisters, let us trustingly invoke their help, as well as the protection of the Guardian Angels whose feast we shall be celebrating (...) on 2 October.
>
> The invisible presence of these blessed spirits is a great help and comfort to us; they walk beside us and protect us in every circumstance, they defend us from danger and we may have recourse to them at every moment.[3]

He again referred to invoking their help in March of 2009.

> Dear brothers and sisters, we would be removing an important part of the Gospel were we to leave out these beings sent by God, who announce and are a sign of his presence among us. Let us invoke them frequently, so that they may sustain us in our commitment to follow Jesus to the point of identifying with him. Let us ask them, especially today, to watch over me and my collaborators in the Roman Curia; this afternoon we shall be beginning a week of

---

[3] BENEDICT XVI, September 29, 2008.

Spiritual Exercises, as we do every year. Mary, Queen of Angels, pray for us![4]

Some people today may inquire what the basis and foundation was for Pope Benedict XVI's comments – How does the Pope discern these teachings? How can the Church teach as strongly and securely about these invisible creatures as Pope Paul VI did?[5] Sacred Scripture is only one reference where one can learn about the spiritual and invisible world. The Holy Father refers to Tradition and the millennium-long experience of the Church as other references for learning. He continued saying:

> Many saints cultivated a rapport of true friendship with the Angels, and numerous episodes testify to their assistance on specific occasions.
>
> Angels are sent by God "to serve, for the sake of those who are to obtain salvation" as the Letter to the Hebrews (1:14) recalls, and are therefore a valuable help to us on our earthly pilgrimage towards the heavenly homeland.[6]

---

[4] BENEDICT XVI, March 1, 2009.

[5] "We believe in one only God, Father, Son and Holy Spirit, creator of things visible such as this world in which our transient life passes, of things invisible such as the pure spirits which are also called angels, and creator in each man of his spiritual and immortal soul" (Paul VI, Apostolic letter *Credo of the People of God*, 1968, 8; cf. Marcello STANZIONE, *I Papi e gli angeli*, Gribaudi Ed., Milano 2010).

[6] BENEDICT XVI, September 29, 2008.

This little work intends to look into *"the 'lived theology' of the saints"*. For, as Saint John Paul II said:

> The saints offer us precious insights which enable us to understand more easily the intuition of faith, thanks to the special enlightenment which some of them have received from the Holy Spirit, or even through their personal experience of those terrible states of trial which the mystical tradition describes as the "dark night".[7]

The Saint chosen for this work is one from recent times, Saint Faustina Kowalska (1905-1938).

---

[7] St. JOHN PAUL II, **Apostolic** Letter « *Novo Millennio Ineunte* » - *At the close of the great Jubilee of the Year 2000*, 2001, 27. For further studies on the good and fallen angels see the following historical studies with rich bibliographies: For the entire history: Renzo LAVATORI, *Gli Angeli. Storia e pensiero*, Casa Editrice Marietti, Genova 1991; Id., *Satana. Un caso serio. Studio di demonologia cristiana*, Centro editoriale dehoniano, Bologna 1996; for the twentieth century: Ignacio M. SUÁREZ RICONDO, *Discusión teológica sobre los Ángeles y los demonios en el siglo XX*, La Stampa S.A., Buenos Aires 2008.

0.2 THE PRESENCE OF THE ANGELS IN THE LIFE OF FAUSTINA KOWALSKA BEFORE ENTERING THE CONVENT

0.2.1 AT HOME WITH HER FAMILY

Our Saint "cultivated a rapport of true friendship with the Angels" to the point that she could say "My communing is with the angels"[8].

St. Faustina's family was very simple. The saint's father always struggled to provide for his family. They lived in the country, far from the city, so they did not participate much in public life, except in the life of the Church. Saint Faustina's father's faith was not only strong doctrinally but also in practice. He sang the office of our Lady early each morning. When one day his wife reminded him of the children who were still sleeping, he responded, "First God! I have to give the little ones a good example"[9].

We can presume that the family included the devotion to the Guardian Angels in their regular devotions, as every good Christian home did during that time. However, it is also possible that their devotion did not go beyond the recitation of the traditional Guardian Angel prayer:

---

[8] Sister M. Faustina KOWALSKA, *Divine Mercy In My Soul. Diary*, Marian Press, Stockbridge, MA, 3rd edition with revisions (28th printing): 2012, 1200. Here after will be referred to by D. and the corresponding number given in this text.

[9] Cf. Maria WINOWSKA, *Anrecht auf Barmherzigkeit*, Paulus Verlag, Freiburg Schweiz 1972, 25.

Angel of God, my Guardian dear,
To whom God's love commits me here,
Ever this day be at my side
To light and guard, to rule and guide.[10]

Sister Sophia Michalenko reports the following reference in the biography she wrote on Saint Faustina.

> Many times, even before the age of seven, the child would awaken during the night and sit up in bed. Her mother could see that she was praying. To put an end to such extraordinary zeal she would say to her, "Go back to sleep or you'll lose your mind." "Oh, no, Mother," Helenka – this was the Baptismal name of Saint Faustina – would answer, "my Guardian Angel must be waking me to pray".[11]

This moment illustrates that the Saint must have grown up aware of her Guardian Angel and of his personal help.

0.2.2 MEMBER OF THE RELIGIOUS INSTITUTE

In 1925 Saint Faustina entered the Congregation of Our Lady of Mercy, the order specified to her by Our Lord. Possessing a more explicit devotion to the Angels than other communities, the

---

[10] Cf. *Handbook of Indulgencies*, Catholic Book Publishing CO, New York, N.Y. 1991, 8; here according the traditional translation.

[11] Sophia MICHALENKO, *Mercy My Mission. Life of Sister Faustina H. Kowalska*, S.M.D.M., Marian Press, Stockbridge, MA 1987, 4.

Congregation designated the Guardian Angel as one of its patron saints. This special devotion led to this custom: daily, at the hour of the Evening Prayer, the local communities implored God to protect the sisters against the enemy through the mediation of the Guardian Angels.

A prayer book of this Congregation from the year 1931 contains a Rosary of Saint Michael, another patron Saint of this religious Congregation. Additionally, the book contains a Litany in his honor.

One convent of this Congregation was dedicated to the Guardian Angels. Saint Faustina stayed in that particular house for some months during 1930, but she did not write any specific comments about the holy Angels during that time.[12]

0.3 THE ANGELOLOGY IN THE DIARY OF SAINT FAUSTINA

In addition to some letters and sheets, Saint Faustina left a spiritual book, her *Diary*. It was written under the orientation of her spiritual director, the Blessed Father Michael Sopocko. It is a significant fact that there are more than 100 references in the Diary to the holy Angels and at least 70 references to the fallen angels.

What inspired Faustina to write so much about the Angels? What importance do these references have in all of her life, writings and mission?

---

[12] Cf. Ibid., 30.

The characteristics of her involvement in her family life, until she became a Postulant in 1925, allows one to see how little she was formed by theologians, or inspired by pious practices of Saints or by any important influence from outside. One of the religious sisters affirms this when commenting: "This girl without talents, without formation, that barely knew how to read and write, that did not learn a profession, had one miserable dress, was certainly not an interesting candidate."[13]

Another sister from the Congregation who was responsible for the preparations for the process of beatification, did not know about any special influence; she commented:

> Sister Faustina never read the "*The Story of a Soul*" of the Little Flower. She never knew the works of Saint John of the Cross and of Saint Theresa of Avila. She never had a Missal... She had only a *New Testament*; her preferred reading was a Biography of Sister Benigna Consolata Ferrero, which stimulated her zeal, but did not enrich her knowledge of the doctrine.[14]

On one occasion, Saint Faustina herself referred to her contact with the world around her:

> I demand nothing from creatures and communicate with them only in so far as is necessary. I will not take them into my confidence unless this is for the greater glory of

---

[13] WINOWSKA, 33 (translation is ours).
[14] WINOWSKA, 46 (translation is ours).

God. My communing is with the angels (D. 1200; of course, Angels are also creatures as St. Faustina makes clear in D. 1741 and elsewhere).

The exclusion of all outside influences is very significant in understanding what she lived as well as what she wrote about the Angels, since it can then be said that almost all her notes about the angelic world are based either on concrete experiences or on deductions from these experiences. At the same time, as a daughter of the Church which she calls "mother" (D. 197), she followed the orientations of the Church so that her personal faith is united with that of the Church with regard to the Angels.

In this regard it is opportune to clarify well: The role of the "private revelations" "is not to 'complete' Christ's definitive revelation, but to help live more fully by it in a certain period of history," as "the value of private revelations is essentially different from that of the one public revelation." Thus, "Ecclesiastical approval of a private revelation essentially means that its message contains nothing contrary to faith and morals." In this way, this revelation "can be a valuable aid for better understanding and living the Gospel at a certain time; consequently it should not be treated lightly".[15]

This can be observed and applied without doubt to the case of Saint Faustina Kowalska

---

[15] BENEDICT XVI, *Post-Synodal Apostolic Exhortation The Word of the Lord - Verbum Domini*, 2010, 14.

whose life and work became a positive contribution for the contemporary Church and the world, a grace of the Holy Spirit (cf. Jn 14:26).

With the vivid desire to fulfill only the will of God and not to offend Him, Saint Faustina could become a fitting instrument in His hands for the Work of the Divine Mercy. Thus, she was conformed to the holy Angels, who are nothing more than servants of the Lord. They appear and act when God asks them. Moreover, in all they do, they reflect only God's greatness, holiness and will.

With the spirit of docility to the divine plans for her life, Saint Faustina was graced by the constant presence and illumination of the holy Angels, that is, of those who contribute constantly, in the world and in history, to God's glorification and men's salvation.

How will we proceed in the presentation of the testimony which this Saint gave of the invisible angelic world?

Since we are using such a rich source, the material will be organized in a way that it serves as an *introduction into the world of the Angels*, the good ones and the fallen ones.

The first chapter will take a short look at the presence of the Angels in the life of Saint Faustina.

The second chapter will include the Angels in their relationship with God, the test and division of the faithful and the fallen Angels.

The third chapter contains excerpts from Saint Faustina's *Diary* about the reign of the Angels and their hierarchy, and about individual Angels and their manifestations toward man.

This leads to the serious question of the mystery of God's love for man and the relation of the Angels towards it. According to the notes in the *Diary* it is possible to learn about the center of the economy of salvation and about four steps in its development; this will be presented in the fourth chapter.

A fifth chapter will pay special attention to the help which man can receive from the Angels, especially from the Guardian Angel, according to the experience of Saint Faustina.

In the sixth and last chapter, a quite complete "demonology" will be presented with different confrontations with the fallen angels. Her rich experiences and their descriptions relate how the devils approach man and tempt him. Saint Faustina also gives many counsels on how to defend oneself against the fallen spirits; these suggestions are of greatest value.

Therefore, we can come to the conviction that through the *Diary* of Saint Faustina, the Church received, from a simple and young Sister behind the walls of a convent, a "*lived theology*," a complete and trustworthy Angelology and Demonology. May she find many listeners and still more imitators.

O Mary, my Mother and my Lady, I offer You my soul, my body, my life and my death, and all that will follow it. I place everything in your hands. O my Mother, cover me with Your virginal mantle and grant me the grace of purity of heart, soul and body. Defend me with Your power against all enemies, and especially against those who hide their malice behind the mask of virtue. O lovely lily! You are for me a mirror, O my Mother! (D. 79)

1. THE PRESENCE OF THE ANGELS IN THE LIFE OF SAINT FAUSTINA

Saint Faustina received many special graces from Jesus, her Divine Redeemer and Spouse. Jesus and Saint Faustina were very close to each other. Despite this relationship, she never closed her soul to the presence and help of Our Lady, of the Saints, and the holy Angels, particularly her Guardian Angel. In her *Diary* she refers many times to the pure spirits, to the holy spirits who are faithful to God, and also to the fallen spirits, who removed themselves from God and are His enemies.

This opening chapter will cover the Angels, good and bad, who were always present in Saint Faustina's daily life. The information will be limited to what is known through her autobiography, *The Diary – Divine Mercy in My Soul*, notes about her interior life, beginning with her entrance into the convent in the year 1925.

1.1 THE GUARDIAN ANGEL

Saint Faustina recalls having received a call to the Consecrated life at the age of seven. She was able to follow the call, with the help of Jesus, when she reached the age of eighteen (cf. D. 7-15). By this time she had matured enough in the spiritual life to give herself totally to God. For this reason, she did not consider that anything happened "by chance". She was conscious that she had to see the "finger" of GOD even behind the little things.

Illuminated by seeing the Providence of God in all things, she also recognized the fact that she entered the convent the day before the Feast of Our Lady of the Angels, August 2nd.

> At last the time came when the door of the convent was opened for me - it was the first of August [1925], in the evening, the vigil [of the feast] of Our Lady of the Angels. I felt immensely happy; it seemed to me that I had stepped into the life of Paradise (D. 17).

Already at the very beginning of her life as a religious, Saint Faustina speaks of a Vision of her Guardian Angel.

> Shortly after this, I fell ill [general exhaustion]. The dear Mother Superior sent me with two other sisters for a rest to Skolimow, not far from Warsaw. It was at that time that I asked the Lord for whom else should I pray for. Jesus said that on the following night He would let me know for whom I should pray.
>
> [The next night] I saw my Guardian Angel, who ordered me to follow him (D. 20).

Saint Faustina prayed to God, and He responded through her Guardian Angel. Therefore it can be said that Saint Faustina's Angel was sent by God. In this way, she learned to deal with her Guardian Angel, who does not offend God, since the Angel, sent as a "servant of the Lord," is faithful to Him before anything else. There is no competition between the holy Angels and God.

Conscious of this attitude of service and fidelity of the Guardian Angel, Saint Faustina began to live with her Guardian Angel in a very natural way: for example, in the manner in which she prepared for her retreat:

> I prepared with great care and prayed long to the Holy Spirit that He might deign to grant me His light and take me under His special guidance: [I prayed] also to Our Lady, to my Guardian Angel, and to our patron saints (D. 1174).

The Angel helped Saint Faustina not only in religious matters, but also in ordinary life. For example, when traveling, she could sometimes concretely verify the visible presence and protection of her Guardian Angel.

> I saw my Guardian Angel, who accompanied me throughout the journey as far as Warsaw. He disappeared when we entered the convent gate. ...

> When we took our seats on the train from Warsaw to Cracow, I once again saw my Guardian Angel at my side. He was absorbed in prayer and in contemplating God, and I followed him with my thoughts. When we arrived at the convent entrance, he disappeared (D. 490).

Because of her call to a great mission, the fallen spirits clearly hated her. Their anger and attacks were prevalent in the life of Saint Faustina.

Satan has admitted to me that I am the object of his hatred. He said that "a thousand souls do me less harm than you do when you speak of the great mercy of the Almighty One. The greatest sinners regain confidence and return to God, and I lose everything. But what is more, you persecute me personally with that unfathomable mercy of the Almighty One" (D. 1167).

She further comments:

I took note of the great hatred Satan has for the Mercy of God. He does not want to acknowledge that God is good (D. 1167; cf. D. 741).

Saint Faustina also received the assistance and help of her Guardian Angel in the spiritual battles with the devil.

When the sermon was over, I did not wait for the end of the service, as I was in a hurry to get back home. When I had taken a few steps, a great multitude of demons blocked my way. They threatened me with terrible tortures, and voices could be heard: "She has snatched away everything we have worked for over so many years!"...

Seeing their great hatred for me, I immediately asked my Guardian Angel for help, and at once the bright and radiant figure of my Guardian Angel appeared and said to me, "Do not fear, spouse of my Lord; without His permission these spirits will do you no harm." Immediately the evil spirits vanished, and the faithful

Guardian Angel accompanied me, in a visible manner, right to the very house (D. 418-419).

On another occasion she needed to make a great renunciation: "I could not even go to Holy Mass or receive Holy Communion today" (D. 1202). She surrendered this to God, and "kept on repeating, 'May the Lord's will be done. I know that Your bounty is without limit'" (ibid.). After this, she tells about the help she received from an Angel. She does not know if the help came from her own Guardian Angel or from another Angel.

> Then I heard an Angel who sang out my whole life history and everything it comprised. I was surprised, but also strengthened (ibid.).

This is a beautiful example of the Christian faith in the holy Angels, who care for the life of men "and protect every human being" (CCC 352). To effectively watch over their charges, they need always to be present: only in this way do they become testimonies of both the good performed and the evil practiced, and present a defense before the throne of God at the end of life, at the particular judgment of the person whom they guarded,[16] and also at the universal judgment.[17]

---

[16] Cf. *Lk* 16:22; *Heb* 9:27; CCC 335; 1021-1022; D. 1565 and 1791; J. DANIELOU, *The Angels and their Mission*, Christian Classics, Allen Tx, ³1996, ch. 9 and 10, 95-114.

[17] Cf. *Mt* 13:39,41,49; 16:27; 24:31; 25:31; *Mk* 8:38; *Lk* 9:26; *1Thess* 4:15-17; *2Thess* 1:7; CCC 1038-1041; Saint JOHN PAUL II, *Catechesis on the Angels*, July 30, 1986: "Creator of Things Unseen - the Angels", 4, in: *God, Father and Creator*, Pauline Books & Media, Boston, MA, 1996, 298-300, 300.

Our Lord's promises in Sacred Scripture became a reality in the life of Saint Faustina, the Secretary of Mercy.

"In my misfortune I called, the Lord heard and saved me from all distress. The Angel of the Lord, who encamps with them, delivers all who fear God. Learn to savor how good the Lord is; happy are those who take refuge in him" (*Ps* 34:7-9).

"Though a thousand fall at your side, ten thousand at your right hand, near you it shall not come. ... For God commands the Angels to guard you in all your ways. With their hands they shall support you, lest you strike your foot against a stone. You shall tread upon the asp and the viper, trample the lion and the dragon" (*Ps* 91:7,11-13).

1.2 THE CONSECRATION OF FAUSTINA AND THE ANGELS

Saint Faustina's familiarity with her Guardian Angel stimulated in her soul the confidence and promptness to take refuge with all the choirs of Angels not only in moments of need, but even more to serve, glorify, love and praise God in a more perfect and pleasing way. When she was alone "one minute before the Blessed Sacrament," she was aware that the holy Angels were with her. Therefore, she prayed with these words:

> O my eternal Lord and Creator, how am I going to thank You for this great favor; namely, that You have deigned to choose miserable me to be Your betrothed and that You are to unite me to yourself in an eternal bond? O dearest Treasure of my heart, I offer You all the adoration and thanksgiving of the Saints and of all the choirs of Angels, and I unite myself in a special way with Your Mother (D. 220).

Saint Faustina sensed this need even more strongly on special days, such as on the day of her *perpetual vows*, when she remembered all creatures including the holy Angels.

> I had asked heaven and earth and had called upon all beings to thank God for this immense and inconceivable favor of His (D. 238).

Later, at the renewal of her vows, she prayed with the same spirit.

> I called upon all heaven and earth to join me in my act of thanksgiving (D. 1369).

In a similar way, she later formulated her great act of offering with the consciousness that she stood in the presence of the Angels.

> Before heaven and earth, before all the choirs of Angels, before the Most Holy Virgin Mary, before all the powers of heaven, I declare to the One Triune God that today, in union with Jesus Christ, Redeemer of souls, I make a voluntary offering of myself for the conversion of sinners, especially for those souls who have lost hope in God's mercy... (D. 309; cf. D. 1680).

1.3 THE ANGELS AND THEIR COMPANIONSHIP, INTERCESSION AND PROTECTION

Saint Faustina asked the holy Angels' help to praise God and give Him thanks in a more intense and worthy manner. She also united herself to the heavenly spirits for the intercessions for men.

Of one of these moments of "*night-adoration on Thursdays*", she tells:

> I made my hour of adoration from eleven o'clock till midnight.... I called upon the whole of heaven to join me in making amends to the Lord for the ingratitude of certain souls.[18]

She turned to the holy Angels in a very natural way. It can be found that God sent them to her in a similar natural manner, without her express

---

[18] D. 319; cf. Bl. DINA BÉLANGER, *Autobiography*, Sillery (Québec) (1934), ⁵1995, ch. 24, on June 5, 1925.

request for their presence. Once, in a specific situation of daily life, Saint Faustina realized that she would be in great danger, and she turned to the Lord with confidence. The immediate response of the Lord was these words:

My daughter, the moment you went to the gate I set a Cherub over it to guard it. Be at peace (D. 1271).

He had already taken care of her and had sent angelic help even before she had started her prayer for aid.

The help came from a member of the second choir of Angels, a Cherub!

On another occasion, Saint Faustina received enormous help from one of the Seraphim: he brought her "the Lord of the Angels," the Eucharistic Jesus, for thirteen days (cf. D. 1676, 1677).

Saint Michael the Archangel particularly stands out in the spirituality of Saint Faustina. She developed a special devotion to Saint Michael, not out of fear of the devil, but out of admiration for the virtues of the Archangel.

I have great reverence for Saint Michael the Archangel; he had no example to follow in doing the will of God, and yet he fulfilled God's will faithfully (D. 667).

She was aware that Saint Michael had to make a decision all by himself during the test of the Angels. He could not imitate or follow anyone. In this isolation, he turned to the Majesty of God –

"Who is like God!" – and humbled himself before His plan. He won and saved himself in this remarkable way.

After she renounced the refuge of creatures, Saint Faustina enjoyed the angelic company.

> I demand nothing from creatures and communicate with them only in so far as is necessary... My communing is with the angels [cf. *Mt.* 18:10; *Ex.* 23:20] (D. 1200; note again, angels are also creatures for St. Faustina, cf. D. 1741 etc.).

In this way, she almost literally realized in her life what the *Imitation of Christ* expresses as a principle of spiritual life, "God and His holy angels will draw near to him who withdraws from friends and acquaintances"[19].

Once, when she went to Warsaw, God allowed her to contemplate an Angel who was always with her. At the same time she could see the Angels who took care of the different churches located on the route. Through this experience, she was able to see a sign of God's benevolence.

---

[19] THOMAS A KEMPIS, *Imitation of Christ*, book I, ch. 20; cf. also Saint Thomas Aquinas in his reflections on the Spiritual Life: "The other is man's spiritual life in respect of his mind, and with regard to this life there is fellowship between us and both God and the angels, imperfectly indeed in this present state of life, wherefore it is written (Phil. 3:20): 'Our conversation is in heaven.' But this 'conversation' will be perfected in heaven, when 'His servants shall serve Him, and they shall see His face' (*Apoc.* 22:3,4)" (St. THOMAS AQ., *Summa Theologiae*, p. II-II, q. 23, a. 1 ad 1).

> I thanked God for His goodness, that He gives us angels for companions. Oh, how little people reflect on the fact that they always have beside them such a guest... ! (D. 630).

During the treatment of her delicate health from 1936 to 1937, Saint Faustina expressed her "last desire" in this life.

> O bright and clear day on which all my dreams will be fulfilled; O day so eagerly desired, the last day of my life! ... O great day, on which divine love will be confirmed in me. On that day, for the first time, I shall sing before heaven and earth the song of the Lord's fathomless mercy (D. 825).

For Saint Faustina, the day of her death would be the day of the testimony of the Mercy of God before the Angels and the Saints. Even the Church prays in these words:

> O God, who in your unfathomable providence are pleased to send your holy Angels to guard us, hear our supplication as we cry to you, that we may always be defended by *their protection and rejoice eternally in their company*. Through our Lord Jesus Christ, your Son, who lives and reigns with you in the unity of the Holy Spirit, one God, for ever and ever. Amen.[20]

---

[20] ROMAN MISSAL, 3rd edition, Collect on October 2.

2. THE ANGELS AND THE DIVINE MERCY

Saint Faustina provides in her writings precious observations of the relationship existing between the holy Angels and the mystery of Divine Mercy. She makes these observations in regard to the origin of the Angels as well as to the answer spiritual creatures give to the God of mercy, in heaven and on earth.

2.1 THE DIVINE ACTION IS MARKED BY MERCY

One of the specific characteristics of Saint Faustina's message is the strong emphasis on the Mercy of God, revealing the biblical and Christian teaching about the importance of this mystery.

2.1.1 ALL WAS CREATED BY DIVINE MERCY

God the Father, "rich in mercy"[21], created in His Son "all things in heaven and on earth, visible and invisible, whether thrones or dominions or principalities or authorities – all things were created through him and for him" (*Col* 1:16).

It is important to state, in all clarity, that God has no need of creatures at all. He is infinitely happy in Himself.

---

[21] *Eph* 2:4 (all biblical quotations are taken from *The Holy Bible. Revised Standard Version. Catholic Edition*, Ignatius Press, San Francisco ⁶1998, except for some Psalms, taken from the *Liturgy of the Hours*, Catholic Book Publishing Company Co., New York, N.Y., 1975; cf. *Lk* 6:36; *2Cor* 1:3; *Heb* 2:17; CCC 211.

> O God, who are happiness in Your very self and have no need of creatures to make You happy, because of Yourself You are the fullness of love (D. 1741).

Considering that God suffices Himself, we can be aware that creation is an act of pure love. Still, contemplating the absolute gratuity with which God creates, and union with Him as the goal for all rational or spiritual creatures, we must recognize the act of creation as an act of the "unfathomable mercy". Therefore all of creation must be attributed not only to the Divine omnipotence, but also to God's mercy.

If I call creatures into being - that is the abyss of My mercy (D. 85; cf. D. 699).

In this way, the holy Angels, the spiritual creatures, reflect the marvelous and powerful Mercy of God, as Saint Faustina explicitly writes:

> All the angels and all humans have emerged from the very depths of Your tender mercy (D. 651),

> For ... out of Your fathomless mercy You call creatures into being ... In Your unfathomable mercy, You have created angelic spirits and admitted them to Your love and to Your divine intimacy (D. 1741).

No creature, not even the most perfect, either has a right to existence, or to such a final and perpetual destiny which God offers them. No one has even the right to determine how to reach it.

On a certain occasion Saint Faustina reflected about the fall of angels. She not only refers to mercy as cause of creation, but also characterizes the time of the Angels before their fall – and before the creation of mankind (cf. CCC 327) – as "time of mercy".

> You did not give the Fallen Angels time to repent or prolong their time of mercy (D. 1489).

2.1.2 THE DIVINE MERCY - INCOMPREHENSIBLE FOR MEN AND ANGELS

In light of these and other facts which faith offers, it can and must be affirmed that Divine Mercy is incomprehensible for any creature, as well as for the Angels. This is what one finds in our Saint's reflections:

> O Incomprehensible God, how great is Your mercy! It surpasses the combined understanding of all men and angels (D. 651).

> Your mercy surpasses the understanding of all Angels and people put together (D. 69).

> **My mercy is so great that no mind, be it of man or of angel, will be able to fathom it throughout all eternity** (D. 699).

> Such is the omnipotence and the miracle of Your mercy. All the tongues of men and of angels united could not find words adequate to this mystery of Your love and mercy (D. 1489).

Yes,

> no mind, either of angel or of man, will ever fathom the mysteries of Your mercy, O God. The angels are lost in amazement before the mystery of divine mercy, but cannot comprehend it.[22]

However, love finds a way: the way of praise and surrender. For this reason Saint Faustina invites us to sing the Litany of Divine Mercy.

> Divine Mercy, unfathomed by any intellect, human or angelic, ... astonishment for Angels ... incomprehensible to Saints, I trust in You (D. 949).

With such a prayer, the souls on earth follow the example of their heavenly protectors and guides.

> O God, this unfathomable mercy enthralls anew all the holy souls and all the spirits of heaven. These pure spirits are immersed in holy amazement as they glorify this inconceivable mercy of God, which in turn arouses even greater admiration in them, and their praise is carried out in a perfect manner (D. 835).

---

[22] D. 1553; cf. D. 492, 819 and 873.

2.2 THE "PARTICIPATION" OF THE ANGELS IN GOD'S PERFECTIONS

Saint Faustina contemplates in the holy Angels a particular attribute of God, who is merciful toward His creatures. The Angels also find themselves in an ecstasy over the other perfections of God. It is impossible to speak about one aspect of God's face and to ignore all the other attributes.

The Saint received from Jesus the necessary instruction about God.

> On one occasion I was reflecting on the Holy Trinity, on the essence of God. I absolutely wanted to know and fathom who God is. ... In an instant my spirit was caught up into what seemed to be the next world. I saw an inaccessible light, and in this light what appeared like three sources of light which I could not understand. And out of that light came words in the form of lightening which encircled heaven and earth. Not understanding anything, I was very sad. Suddenly, from this sea of inaccessible light came our dearly beloved Savior, unutterably beautiful with His shining Wounds. And from this light came a voice which said, **Who God is in His Essence, no one will fathom, neither the mind of Angels nor of man.** Jesus said to me, **Get to know God by contemplating His attributes.** A moment later, He traced the sign of the Cross with His hand and vanished (D. 30).

Saint Faustina speaks about the "participation" of the Angels in the perfections of God.

You have created angelic spirits and admitted them to Your love and to Your divine intimacy. You have made them capable of eternal love. Although You bestowed on them so generously, O Lord, the splendor of love and beauty, Your fullness was not diminished in the least, O God, nor have their love and beauty completed You, because You are everything in Yourself (D. 1741).

She concludes her reflection in this way:

And if You have allowed them to participate in Your happiness and to exist and to love You, that is only due to the abyss of Your mercy. This is Your unfathomable goodness, for which they glorify You without end, humbling themselves at the feet of Your majesty as they chant their eternal hymn: Holy, Holy, Holy ... (ibid.).

All divine attributes are merely expressions of God's essence. Consequently, all of them require creatures to respond to God Himself. Yet, even an answer similar to that made by the holy Angels is insufficient.

My daughter, even if you were to speak at one and the same time in all human and angelic tongues, even then you would not have said very much, but on the contrary, you would have sung in only a small measure the praises of My goodness – of My unfathomable mercy (D. 1605).

The liturgical season of Advent was, for Sister Faustina, a time of special graces for these reflections. In Advent, the liturgy looks at the One God, known in the Old Testament, and sings "To you, I lift up my soul, O my God"[23]. This leads man into a greater revelation.

> During Advent, a great yearning for God arose in my soul. My spirit rushed toward God with all its might. During that time, the Lord gave me much light to know His attributes (D. 180).

> The Saint shares three of these insights.

> The first attribute which the Lord gave me to know is His holiness. His holiness is so great that all the Powers and Virtues tremble before Him. The pure spirits veil their faces and lose themselves in unending adoration, and with one single word they express the highest form of adoration; that is - Holy...

> The second kind of knowledge which the Lord granted me concerns His justice. His justice is so great and penetrating that it reaches deep into the heart of things, and all things stand before Him in naked truth, and nothing can withstand Him.

> The third attribute is love and mercy. And I understood that the greatest attribute is love and mercy (D. 180).

Saint Faustina gives insight into the reaction of the Angels before God and His attributes. Before His Divine Holiness, the holy Angels "tremble"

---

[23] ROMAN MISSAL, Entrance Antiphon on the First Sunday of Advent.

(D. 566), but they also glorify the Lord through the song, proclaiming that He is the "Holy One" as already said by the prophet Isaiah (cf. Is 6:2-4) and the evangelist John (cf. Rev 4:8).

> When during adoration, I repeated the prayer, "Holy God" several times, a vivid presence of God suddenly swept over me, and I was caught up in spirit before the majesty of God. I saw how the Angels and the Saints of the Lord give glory to God. The glory of God is so great that I dare not try to describe it, because I would not be able to do so ... (D. 1604).

Speaking about the Divine Justice, Saint Faustina wrote this:

> Then I saw the Mother of God, who said to me, Oh, how pleasing to God is the soul that follows faithfully the inspirations of His grace! I gave the Savior to the world; as for you, you have to speak to the world about His great mercy and prepare the world for the Second Coming of Him who will come, not as a merciful Savior, but as a just Judge. Oh, how terrible is that day! Determined is the day of justice, the day of divine wrath. The angels tremble before it.[24]

About the Love of God, the Saint says:

---

[24] D. 635. As love does not cancel the truth, so mercy does not annul justice. We can make this conclusion from other paragraphs of the *Diary*, like this one about purgatory: "**My mercy does not want this, but justice demands it.**" (D. 20; cf. CCC 954, 955, 958, 1030-1032).

O Love, O queen! Love knows no fear. It passes through all the choirs of angels that stand on guard before His throne. It will fear no one. It reaches God and is immersed in Him as in its sole treasure. The Cherubim [sic!] who guards paradise with flaming sword, has no power over it. O pure love of God, how great and unequalled you are! (D. 781).

According to Saint Faustina, the Angels are marked by the immensity of God and by their own incapacity to correspond to Him. They sing the eternal "Holy" because they don't know how to respond better.

Be praised, merciful God, One God in the Holy Trinity,
Unfathomable, infinite, incomprehensible,
Immersing themselves in You, their [the Angels'] minds cannot comprehend You,
So they repeat without end their eternal: Holy.

Be glorified, O merciful Creator of ours, O Lord,
Omnipotent, but full of compassion, inconceivable.
To love You is the mission of our existence,
Singing our eternal hymn: Holy ... (D. 1742; cf. D. 361).

God created all creatures for His greater glory.

As purely spiritual creatures angels have intelligence and will: they are personal and immortal creatures, surpassing in perfection all visible creatures, as the splendor of their glory bears witness (CCC 330).

"With their whole beings" (CCC 329) and with Divine assistance, they adore the greatness of God and glorify His splendor.

> I see the angelic choirs giving You honor without cease, and all the heavenly Powers praising You without cease, and without cease they are saying: Holy, Holy, Holy (D. 80).

> The heavens cannot contain Him. The Seraphim who stand closest to Him cover their faces and repeat unceasingly: Holy, Holy, Holy (D. 1805).

> I was carried in spirit before the throne of God. There I saw the heavenly Powers which incessantly praise God (D. 85).

When Saint Faustina remained unsatisfied with the love and praise she was able to offer God,[25] she turned to the holy Angels with admiration: "I admire the singing of the Seraphim, they who are so dearly loved by You" (D. 195.3). She had hoped to grow in her own fervor through the union with them.

> I heard angels singing in various tones, "Holy, Holy, Holy," with chanting so delightful that no human tongue could ever match it (D. 1111).

2.3 THE FALL OF ANGELS

The adoration of the Divine Majesty is an act of love and surrender. This act is also required

---

[25] Besides the "long hours" (D. 195.2) she some times offered God in adoration.

from the Angels and they especially accomplish it, even if they are – and more so precisely because they are – very much closer to God than men. Only God must be adored (cf. *Rev* 19:10) under any attribute: the Omnipotent God, the Holy etc., but principally the Merciful God. Furthermore, it is not important if He is understood or not, because He is always adorable and merits to be adored.

However, not all beings agree on this point. Saint Faustina refers to the rebellion of some Angels against this submission to God. Some did not unite themselves in this song of praise and adoration. The world of the Angels split: some submitted themselves to His Majesty and defended it, while others refused God's plan of love and rebelled against Him.

The Saint speaks about the sin of Lucifer to illustrate the ugliness of any sin against God.

> To receive God's light and recognize what God wants of us and yet not do it is a great offense against the majesty of God. Such a soul deserves to be completely forsaken by God. It resembles Lucifer, who had great light, but did not do God's will (D. 666).

It is difficult to understand this attitude. One knows what God wants, but does not do it. An Angel, even with his clear vision of God and of His love, does not want to fulfill His will. Saint Faustina is still more explicit in another paragraph when she says:

> One of the most beautiful spirits would not recognize Your mercy,
> And, blinded by his pride, he drew others after him.
> Angel of great beauty, he became Satan
> And was cast down in one moment from heaven's heights into hell (D. 1742).

This corresponds to the faith and teaching of the Church which instructs us: The Angels, spiritual creatures, "were indeed created naturally good by God," but some of them "became evil by their own doing" (CCC 391); "indeed, they have sinned" (CCC 311).

Thus, by their "free choice", the devil and the other demons ignored

> God's supremacy, which requires ... an act of docile and obedient subjection. All this summed up concisely in the words: "I will not serve" (Jer 2:20), which manifest the radical and irreversible refusal to take part in the building up of the kingdom of God.[26]

They "have freely refused to serve God and his plan" (CCC 414) and now "act in the world out of hatred for God and his kingdom in Christ Jesus"[27].

---

[26] St. JOHN PAUL II, *Catechesis on the Angels*, July 23, 1986, 5: "Creator of the Angels Who Are Free Beings", in: *God, Father and Creator*, Pauline Books & Media, Boston, MA, 1996, 294-297, 296-297; cf. CCC 392.

[27] CCC 395. The *Catechism of the Catholic Church* (= CCC) refers to the fall of the Angels with reference to the second

Saint Faustina never doubted the existence of these fallen spirits. She wondered:

> As I was meditating on the sin of the Angels and their immediate punishment, I asked Jesus why the Angels had been punished as soon as they had sinned. I heard a voice: **Because of their profound knowledge of God. No person on earth, even though a great saint, has such knowledge of God as an Angel has** (D. 1332).

To "give the Fallen Angels time to repent or prolong their time of mercy" (D. 1489) was not even possible. The Church explains with Saint John Damascene that God could not give them another chance because "for them, after their fall, repentance does not exist as there is not one for men after death" (CCC 393); and this precisely, because Satan – and all the other demons like him – is not willing to repent. "Satan hates mercy more than anything else. It is his greatest torment"[28]. Yet, Saint Faustina heard and recorded this. **"The devils glorify My Justice but do not believe in My Goodness"** (D. 300).

---

letter of St. Peter (2:4, and the parallel *Jd* 6). The Fathers of the Church saw in passages like *Is* 14:4-20 and *Ez* 28:8-10 a reference to this hyper-historical fact, even if the literal meaning may refer to the historical breakdown of the kings of Babylon and of Tyro; cf. St. JOHN PAUL II, *Catechesis on the Angels*, August 13, 1986: "The Fall of the Rebellious Angels" in: *God, Father and Creator*, Pauline Books & Media, Boston, MA, 1996, 307-312; and August 20, 1986: "Christ's Victory Conquers Evil", ibid., 313-317.

[28] D. 764; cf. D. 812; for the parallel to the sins against the Holy Spirit CCC 1864.

On a certain occasion, Saint Faustina saw Saint Michael in the midst of many Angels as an admirable person. Without looking to the right or to the left, he fixed himself only at the truth which he proclaimed: God is faithful, God does not deceive, God wants the good for all! Who is like God?

Many Angels followed the example of Saint Michael.[29]

> Then the faithful spirits cried, "Glory to God's mercy!"
> And they stood firm in spite of the fiery test.
> Glory to Jesus, the Christ abased,
> Glory to His Mother, the humble and pure Virgin.
>
> After this battle, the pure spirits plunged into the ocean of Divinity;
> Contemplating and praising the depths of His mercy,
> They drown in His mercy and manifold light,
> Possessing in knowledge the Trinity of Persons, the Oneness of Godhead (D. 1742; cf. D. 667).

Those men who will achieve heaven will be forever in the company of the adoring Angels. Saint Faustina heard, probably in a conference or homily, the theological thesis that men will occupy in heaven the places of the fallen angels, and therefore, there will be as many saints in heaven as fallen angels in hell.

---

[29] Cf. St. THOMAS AQ., *Summa Theologiae*, p. I, q. 63, a. 8.

O merciful God, ... in Your goodness You grant that human beings may fill the places vacated by the ungrateful angels. O God of great mercy, who turned Your Sacred gaze away from the rebellious angels and turned it upon contrite man, praise and glory be to Your unfathomable mercy, O God who do not despise the lowly heart.[30]

With these holy faithful Angels Saint Faustina sings this hymn:

Be blessed, merciful God, Eternal Love.
You are above the heavens, the sapphires, the firmaments.
Thus the host of pure spirits glorifies You,
With its eternal hymn: Thrice Holy.

And, gazing upon You, face to face, O God,
I see that You could have called other creatures before them.
Therefore they humble themselves before You in great humility,
For well they see that this grace comes solely from Your mercy (D. 1742).

---

[30] D. 1339. That men will occupy the places of the fallen angels in heaven is one of the theories to determine the number of the Angels (cf. for example St. AUGUSTINE, *Enchiridion*, 28-29); however, it seems impossible to know or determine something about the number of the Angels (cf. *Dan* 7:10; *1 Kings* 22:19; *Jb* 25:3; *Lk* 2:13; *Mt* 26:53; *Heb* 12:22; *Rev* 5:11; THOMAS AQ., *Summa Theologiae*, p. I, q. 50, a. 3; P. PARENTE, *The Angels. The Catholic Teaching on the Angels*, TAN, Rockford, IL 1994, 14-18).

3. THE FAITHFUL ANGELS: WHO THEY ARE AND HOW THEY MANIFEST THEMSELVES

The texts we have examined up to this point show various indications about the Angels themselves and their manifestations in the lives of men. It is worthwhile to consider these two aspects separately, especially since the world of the pure spirits is not directly perceptive to human nature.

Saint Faustina speaks little about the homilies she heard, the conferences of preachers, or the instructions she received. But she can speak to us from her own experiences which were granted to her by God.

3.1 THE IDENTITY OF ANGELS

3.1.1 THE DIFFERENT NAMES FOR THE ANGELS
The Saint speaks of the Angels in different terms, using both generic and particular names; her writings require attentive reading.

3.1.1.1 GENERAL NAMES
First of all, it is clear that she speaks of all the holy Angels when she uses the term "heaven": "All heaven catches the flame from You and is filled with love"[31] – or all the "heavens": "The heavens cannot contain Him" (D. 1805).

---

[31] D. 1808; cf. 238, 319 etc.

Equally, it is clear to whom the term "*pure spirits*" refers: "The pure spirits veil their faces and lose themselves in unending adoration" (D. 180).

Also, the reference to choirs is evident: "This great Lord is my Bridegroom. It is to Him that the Choirs sing"[32]. The word "*choir*" refers to all Angels. Saint John Paul II refers to them in his Catechesis:

> The ancient authors and the liturgy itself speak also of the angelic choirs (nine, according to Dionysius the Areopagite) ... Sacred Scripture refers to the Angels also by using terms that are ... "collective" (like the titles: seraphim, cherubim thrones, powers, dominions, principalities), just as it distinguishes between Angels and Archangels. ... these beings and persons, as it were grouped together in society, are divided into orders and grades, corresponding to the measure of their perfection and to their tasks entrusted to them[33].

3.1.1.2 PARTICULAR NAMES

There are texts in the *Diary* in which Saint Faustina mentions certain names of particular choirs; however, these specific terms sometimes refer to all the Angels.

---

[32] D. 1805; cf. D. 80; 161; 220; 309; 761; 781; 1215.

[33] St. JOHN PAUL II, *Catechesis on the Angels*, August 6, 1986: "Angels Participate in History of Salvation", 3, in: *God, Father and Creator*, Pauline Books & Media, Boston, MA, 1996, 301-306, 302.

The first of them is *Angels*. This is the name used most often to indicate all good spirits, faithful to God, as in Psalm 103: "Bless the Lord, O you his Angels, you mighty ones who do his word, hearkening to the voice of his word!"[34] Saint Faustina speaks in this larger sense of all the Angels, for example when she mentions the "Bread of Angels"[35].

In the same generic sense, referring to all the Angels, she speaks of the *Powers*:

> O King of Glory, though You hide Your beauty, yet the eye of my soul rends the veil. I see the angelic choirs giving You honor without cease, and all the heavenly Powers praising You without cease, and without cease they are saying: "Holy, Holy, Holy" (D. 80).

"Powers" is another name for one singular choir of Angels, but through the adjective "heavenly", or through context, it is understood that the Saint is referring at that moment to all the holy Angels, e.g. in the following text:

> On Friday, after Holy Communion, I was carried in spirit before the throne of God. There I saw the heavenly powers which incessantly praise God (D. 85; cf. D. 309).

---

[34] *Ps* 103:20; cf. CCC 329.
[35] D. 1324; cf. CCC 1331; the word "Angels" is used as the specific name for the ninth choir in *Rom* 8:38 or *1Pet* 3:22.

Particularly delicate is the frequent expression of the two choirs, *Powers and Virtues*.[36]

> The first attribute which the Lord gave me to know is His holiness. His holiness is so great that all the Powers and Virtues tremble before Him (D. 180).

In this text and the next, the inclination to refer to them only as particular choirs seems much stronger:

> He is the King of kings, the Lord of lords. Before Him, all power and dominion tremble (D. 1810).

Even so, it is not wrong to think that these choirs are mentioned here in the two senses. It can be said that they characterize the determined choirs, while at the same time, they refer to the Angels as a whole, as *pars pro toto* – a part for all.

In any case, it can be affirmed that all holy Angels are united in the praise of God, or in the words of the *Diary*:

> I saw how the Angels and the Saints of the Lord give glory to God.[37]

---

[36] It is Saint Paul who most often speaks about the hierarchy of the Angels (cf. H. SCHLIER, *Principalities and Powers in the New Testament*, Herder and Herder, New York, NY 1961; P. PARENTE, *The Angels*, 48-55 and 71-82; Henri M. BOUDON, *Devotion to the Nine Choirs of Angels and especially to the Angel-Guardians*, St Athanasius Press, Potosi, MI 2009. The name *Virtues* is missing in the list of eight choirs which Saint John Paul II mentions nominally in his Catechesis.

3.1.2 THE HIERARCHY OF THE ANGELS

Saint Faustina writes clearly about the existence of a hierarchical order among the angelic choirs. She affirms that the Angels praise God according to their capacities, based on their hierarchical order.

> This great majesty of God ... is worshipped by the heavenly spirits according to their degree of grace and the hierarchies into which they are divided.[38]

---

[37] D. 1604. It is worthwhile to note that, every day in the liturgy, the Church wants to unite herself to the song not only of the Seraphim, but of all the Angels, and sing "with Angels and Archangels, with Thrones and Dominions, and with all the hosts and Powers of heaven" (ROMAN MISSAL, "Preface I of Advent"); "Through him the Angels praise your majesty, Dominions adore and Powers tremble before you. Heaven and Virtues of heaven and the blessed Seraphim worship together with exultation" (ibid., "Preface I of the Blessed Virgin Mary"). And the Blessed Trinity "is praised by Angels and Archangels, Cherubim, too, and Seraphim, who never cease to cry out each day, as with one voice they acclaim: Holy, Holy, Holy Lord God" (ibid., "Preface on the Solemnity of the Most Holy Trinity").

[38] D. 779. It seems that Saint John Paul II wanted to confirm the doctrine of Sacred Scripture, Tradition and Liturgy for being so explicit: "Theology, especially in the patristic and medieval periods, has not rejected these representations, seeking to explain them in doctrinal and mystical terms, without, however, attributing an absolute value to them. St. Thomas preferred to deepen his research into the ontological condition, the epistemological activity and will and into the loftiness of these purely spiritual creatures, both because of their dignity in the scale of beings and also because he could

Within the nine choirs, commonly recognized, Saint Faustina refers most frequently to the highest and second-highest in the celestial hierarchy, the Seraphim and Cherubim.

> Two streams in the form of rays
> Have gushed forth from the Heart of Jesus,
> Not for Angels, nor Cherubim, nor Seraphim,
> But for the salvation of sinful man (D. 522).

The prophet Isaiah mentions the following experience of Angels of the first Choir, the *Seraphim*, who are also considered, according to all Tradition, those "who stand closest to Him [God]" (D. 1805).

> In the year that King Uzziah died I saw the Lord sitting upon a throne, high and lifted up; and his train filled the temple. Above him stood the seraphim; each had six wings: with two he covered his face, and with two he covered his feet, and with two he flew. And one called to another and said: "Holy, holy, holy is the Lord of hosts; the whole earth is full of his glory." And the foundations of the thresholds shook at the voice of him who

---

investigate more deeply in them the *capacities and the activities* that are proper to the spirit in the pure state, deducting no little light to illuminate the basic problems that have always agitated and stimulated human thought: knowledge, love, liberty, docility to God, how to reach his kingdom" (St. JOHN PAUL II, *Catechesis on the Angels*, August 6, 1986: "Angels Participate in History of Salvation", in: *God, Father and Creator*, 302-303).

called, and the house was filled with smoke (*Is* 6:1-4; cf. *Rev* 4:8).

Saint Faustina turns to these highest Angels, to those closest to God, with deep respect and with sincere love.

> He is a great Lord, this Bridegroom of mine. The heavens cannot contain Him. The Seraphim who stand closest to Him cover their faces and repeat unceasingly: Holy, Holy, Holy.[39]

The *Cherubim* are principally known as those who protected the doors of Paradise, and through their function to be vigilant over those who ask to have access to the One Who is a Saint:

> O Love, O queen! Love knows no fear, It passes through all the choirs of angels ... reaches God and is immersed in Him as in its sole treasure. The Cherubim who guards [sic!] paradise with flaming sword, has no power over it.[40]

Sister Faustina remembered the first text in Sacred Scripture about the Cherubim. They were mentioned in relation to the fall of man in paradise: God

---

[39] D. 1805. The choir, the Saint most frequently mentions is the *Seraphim*. We can find references to a Seraph or to the entire first choir in the following numbers of the *Diary*: 195, 278, 334, 522, 552, 995, 1049, 1231, 1427, 1632, 1676-1677, 1718, 1735, 1746 and 1805.

[40] D. 781; cf. D. 522, 1022, 1271 and 1632.

"drove out the man; and at the east of the garden of Eden He placed the Cherubim, and a flaming sword which turned every way, to guard the way to the tree of life"[41].

Then we find a reference to the third choir, the choir of the *Thrones*:

This great Lord is my Bridegroom. It is to Him that the Choirs sing. It is before Him that the Thrones bow down. By His splendor the sun is eclipsed (D. 1805).

Including the *Archangels* and *Angels*, the choirs of the *Dominions, Powers* and *Virtues* have already been mentioned (cf. D. 180; 1810). The only choir not explicitly mentioned in the *Diary* is the *Principalities*. However, their identity is clear in Sacred Scripture,[42] and Saint Faustina would have had no motive to ignore or exclude them when she referred, in a wide sense, to the "choirs" of Angels without further specification.

The Saint exclaims once: "What a joy it is to be a faithful child of the Church" (D. 481). The revelations she received did not drive her away from the "deposit of the faith". Rather, through the work of the Holy Spirit, they brought some

---

[41] *Gen* 3:24. Sacred Scripture mentions them almost a hundred times cf. *Ex* 25:18-22; *Ps* 18[17]:10; *Is* 37:16; ... *Heb* 9:5.

[42] Cf. *Eph* 1:21; *Col* 1:16; St. THOMAS AQ., *Summa Theologiae*, p. I., q. 108, especially aa. 5 and 6. Saint Michael, normally considered an Archangel (*Jude* 9), is also called "Prince" (*Dan* 10:13,22; 12:1). Some interpret this as a reference to him as one of the Principalities.

light to the existence of certain groups of Angels, present in the faith of the Church and in the faith of the people of God.

3.1.3 GROUPS OF ANGELS

Beyond a mere reference to the angelic choirs, Saint Faustina also knew about certain "groups of Angels". In 1935, the Saint spoke about a vision of an Angel whom she could not classify into any choir. The Angel himself said that he belongs to a group of seven.

> One day, ... I saw a spirit of great beauty who spoke these words to me: "Don't cry - says the Lord." After a moment I asked, "Who are you?" He answered me, "I am one of the seven spirits who stand before the throne of God day and night and give Him ceaseless praise" (D. 471).

Here two characteristics are given: one of *personal* character – a special beauty which comes from his love and knowledge of God – and another of *social* character – by the fact that he belongs to a specific group. Her remark about the beauty of this Angel will be mentioned again later. The fact that certain Angels form a group of "seven spirits" is already known in Sacred Scripture. Saint Raphael presented himself as such in the Old Testament:

> "I am Raphael, *one of the seven* holy Angels who present the prayers of the saints and enter into the presence of the glory of the Holy One" (Tb 12:15).

Further, Saint John, the apostle, mentions different groups in his *Book of Revelation*.[43]

3.1.4 *INDIVIDUAL ANGELS*

Besides the references to the choirs and to groups, the *Diary* of Saint Faustina includes explicit references to individual Angels. *Explicit* because each Angel, be it a Seraph, a Cherub, or a member of an angelic group, is always an individual person.

Saint Faustina "heard the voice of an angel" who was about to cause a damaging storm and "the angel's complaint to God" (D. 1791).

More impressive was the vision of the *Angel who will execute the divine wrath*. He is not necessarily the same one who freed Israel from Egypt. However, aside from this incident, Sacred Scripture does not give a description of him to the extent given here.[44]

> I saw an Angel, the executor of divine wrath. He was clothed in a dazzling robe, his face gloriously bright, a cloud beneath his feet. From the cloud, bolts of thunder and flashes of

---

[43] Cf. *Rev* 2-3; 6:2ff; 8:2ff; 16:2ff. Pope Benedict XVI observed "that in the ancient Church - already in the Book of Revelation - Bishops were described as 'angels' of their Church, thereby expressing a close connection between the Bishop's ministry and the Angel's mission" (Homily, September 29, 2007; there are more than 70 references to Angels in the total Book of Revelation).

[44] Cf. *Gen* 19:13; *2Sam* 24:16-17; *Dan* 13:55,59; *Acts* 12:23; *1Cor* 10:10; *Rev* 16. About this theme, see more below, chapter 4.5.

lightning were springing into his hands; and from his hand they were going forth, and only then were they striking the earth (D. 474).

Of the three Archangels, Saint Faustina refers just to one, *Saint Michael*. "Saint Michael the Archangel, I saw by my side that great Leader, who spoke ... to me" and "I feel his presence and assistance"[45].

Her *Guardian Angel* is another individual Angel whom she mentions, with whom she speaks; illustrations of this will be mentioned later (see below chapter 5.2).

---

[45] D. 706; cf. D. 480 and 667. Sacred Scripture and Tradition reveal us the name of only three Angels: Gabriel (*Dan* 8:16; 9:21; *Lk* 1:19,26), Michael (*Dan* 10:13,21; 12:1; *Jude* 9; *Rev* 12:7) and Raphael (*Tb* 3:17; 12:15). The Apocryphal books indicate more names of Angels; however, their origin can not be verified. The Church limited herself to the three names mentioned and does not want other names to be used, nor Angels to be venerated under other names. This is affirmed different times in history as on the Council of Laodiceia de Frigia (ca. 360 AD; cân. 35) or at the Synod of Rome (in the year 745 under Pope Zacarias). The names which appeared on the image of Our Lady of the Angels in the Basílica Maria degli Angeli in Rome needed to be covered (cf. BENEDICT XIV, "The Angels and their Cult", in: *Doctrina de Beatificatione*, lib IV, p. II, chap. 30, n. 3). In our times, the Church made another step saying: "The practice of assigning names to the Holy Angels should be discouraged, except in the cases of Gabriel, Raphael and Michael whose names are contained in Holy Scripture" (CONGREGATION FOR DIVINE WORSHIP AND THE DISCIPLINE OF THE SACRAMENTS, *Directory on Popular Piety and the Liturgy. Principles and Guidelines*, 2001, 217).

A less familiar case is an individual Angel who is only identified by his work: He has to take care of a church.

> When I was riding on the train, I saw an Angel standing on every church we passed, but surrounded by a light which was paler than that of the spirit who was accompanying me on the journey, and each of these spirits who were guarding the churches bowed his head to the spirit who was near me (D. 630).

What can be said about this text?

First, the task of an Angel coincides with what Saint Augustine and, after him, Saint Thomas Aquinas teach, namely that "all corporeal things [are] ruled by the Angels"[46].

Second, there is not just *one* Angel for all the churches, but it seems that *each* church has its spiritual Guardian, for Saint Faustina says "each of these spirits who were guarding the churches ...."

A third observation has to be made about the different luminosity Saint Faustina observed: "but surrounded by a light which was paler than that of the spirit who was accompanying me on the journey". This light indicates, very probably, the place which this Angel occupies in the angelic hierarchy. If this is the case, then the Guardian Angel of Saint Faustina, or, more precisely, the Angel "who was accompanying [her] on the journey," would come from a higher choir than

---

[46] St. THOMAS AQ., *Summa Theologiae*, p. I, q. 110, a. 1c.

those Angels who watched over the churches. The higher or closer to God a creature is, the more brilliantly it is manifested. Saint John of the Cross explains the communication among the Angels in this way:

> Ordinarily these works and inspirations are derived from God by means of the Angels, and the Angels also in turn give them one to another without delay. This communication is like that of a ray of sunlight shining through many windows placed one after the other. Although it is true that of itself the ray of light passes through them all, nevertheless each window communicates this light to the other with a certain modification according to its own quality. The communication is more or less intense insofar as the window is closer to or farther from the sun.[47]

When observing men, it can be seen that some persons are gifted with a certain charisma and are capable of transmitting special beauty, light, or strength to its surrounding. Something similar can be found with the Angels according to the choir they belong to. On the natural level, it is the mystery of participation of the creatures, capable of knowledge and love; however, on the supernatural dimension, it is the mystery of the divine presence, grace, and beauty.

---

[47] St. JOHN OF THE CROSS, *The Dark Night*, Washington, DC 1979, II, XII.3.

3.2 THE MANIFESTATIONS OF THE ANGELS TO SAINT FAUSTINA

Different forms of the angelic manifestations can be found in the *Diary* of Saint Faustina. What she underlines in a special way is the effects that they cause in men, the "fruits" according to which one has to examine and discern the spirits.[48] Of that *spirit of great beauty* whom our Saint saw, she affirmed: "his beauty comes from close union with God". At the same time she declared about him also, "This spirit does not leave me for a single moment, but accompanies me everywhere" (D. 471).

This observation is not reason enough to affirm that it is her Guardian Angel; but it serves to indicate another dimension of the Angels. They are not only oriented towards God or towards the union with Him which is certainly their principal goal, but also have, simultaneously, a task related with human creatures as the author of the Letter to the Hebrews teaches: "Are they not all ministering spirits sent forth to serve, for the sake of those who are to obtain salvation?" (*Heb* 1:14) In this light, Pope Benedict XVI pointed out this mystery which is so significant for the ministers of God:

> Pope Gregory the Great, in one of his homilies, once said that God's Angels, however far afield they go on their missions, always move in God. They remain always with Him. And while speaking about the Angels, Saint Gregory thought also of bishops and priests:

---

[48] Cf. *Mt* 7:16-20; *Gal* 5:22; *Eph* 5:9-10; *1Thess* 5:21; *1Jn* 4:1.

wherever they go, they should always "be with Him".[49]

The Seraphim's proximity to God is manifested through the splendor which does not cause fear but confidence and peace.

> The Seraph was surrounded by a great light, the divinity and love of God being reflected in him. He wore a golden robe and, over it, a transparent surplice and a transparent stole. The chalice was crystal, covered with a transparent veil (D. 1676).

Once, the Lord said to Saint Faustina that He placed a Cherub at the gate of the Convent to guard it; therefore He asked her to "Be at peace".

> After returning from my conversation with the Lord, I saw a little white cloud and, in it, a Cherub with his hands joined. His gaze was like lightening, and I understood how the fire of God's love burns in that look ... (D. 1271).

This image convinced the Sister that she was well protected. In that moment there was no danger and if danger were to come, the Angel would take care of all.

Sister perceived also positive effects: a sensation of beauty and power, peace and especially a longing for heaven! Such is her description:

> I saw a spirit of great beauty ... this spirit did not soothe my yearning, but roused me to even

---

[49] BENEDICT XVI, Homily on September 11, 2006.

greater longing for God. This spirit is very beautiful, and his beauty comes from close union with God ... His voice was like that of a thousand voices; it is impossible to put it into words (D. 471).

This majestic figure recalls the visions of the Angels in Sacred Scripture. Saint John, the evangelist, describes, for example, one of his mysterious visions with words similar to those of the prophet Daniel (cf. *Dan* 10:5-6) and Ezekiel (cf. *Ez* 8:2-3):

Then I saw another mighty Angel coming down from heaven, wrapped in a cloud, with a rainbow over his head, and his face was like the sun, and his legs like pillars of fire. He had a little scroll open in his hand. And he set his right foot on the sea, and his left foot on the land, and called out with a loud voice, like a lion roaring; when he called out, the seven thunders sounded (*Rev* 10:1-3).

It is clear what is essential and constant in reference to the holy Angels. They reflect the Glory of God and are totally dedicated to His praise and adoration. This is also true for the Guardian Angels.

I once again saw my Guardian Angel at my side. He was absorbed in prayer and in contemplating God, and I followed him with my thoughts (D. 490).

The Angels also serve men. This is more evident in relation to the Guardian Angel, the Angel who is more constantly close to the human being.[50] The following apparition shows this very well:

> ... the bright and radiant figure of my Guardian Angel appeared and ... accompanied me, in a visible manner, right to the very house. His look was modest and peaceful, and a flame of fire sparkled from his forehead (D. 419; cf. D. 471).

In relation to those whom they serve, the Guardian Angels act like good instruments of the Holy Spirit, consoling, illuminating, encouraging and protecting. "Perfect love casts out fear" (*1Jn* 4:18; cf. *Gal* 5:22-23). Therefore Jesus exhorted the disciples constantly "Have no fear" (*Mt* 14:27), and so did, for example, "the Angel of the Lord" who appeared to St. Joseph, "Do not fear ..."[51]. This encouragement is found also on the lips of the Guardian Angel of Saint Faustina, and certainly also on the lips of the Guardian Angel of every one, as they are faithful followers of the Son of God: "Do not fear, spouse of my Lord" (D. 419).

To consider and esteem truly this communication of the Angels with men it is necessary to consider the illustrations this Saint presents of the humility of the Angels and the preference which God gave to the human race.

---

[50] Cf. St. THOMAS AQ., *Summa Theologiae*, p. I, q. 113, a. 3.
[51] *Mt* 1:20; cf. *Dan* 10:12; *Lk* 1:13,30; 2:10 and others.

4. THE PREFERENCE OF GOD FOR MEN

Saint Faustina wrote these words of Jesus in her *Diary*:

> **My beloved child, delight of My Heart, your words are dearer and more pleasing to Me than the angelic chorus. All the treasures of My Heart are open to you** (D. 1489.11).

In the previous chapter, we observed the greatness and holiness of the Angels, as well as the beauty of their hymns and praises. After these revelations, it is surprising to read that a human being, gifted with a body and spirit and marked by weaknesses and idiosyncrasies, is more pleasing to our Lord than those who stand forever in His presence.

> **Beloved pearl of My Heart, I see your love so pure, purer than that of the angels, and all the more so because you keep on fighting. For your sake I bless the world** (D. 1061).

> ... nothing can disturb my close union with Him, not even the angelic powers.[52]

Her ardent love places her above the Angels! Saint Faustina herself is admired, because of this singular preference, and she prays in this way:

> O God of great mercy, who turned Your sacred gaze away from the rebellious angels and turned it upon contrite man (D. 1339; cf. D. 1489.5-6).

---

[52] D. 1135; cf. D. 686, 745.

On the feast of Saint Agnes, the Virgin Martyr, Holy Church uses an antiphon that also expresses a preference for human beings by God. The Angels are described as servants, while the holy young lady is found much closer to Him: "I am *espoused* to Him whom the Angels *serve*"[53].

Saint Faustina, then, was inspired by this idea that God prefers men to angels.

4.1 GOD'S MERCY AND THE INCARNATION

4.1.1 THE REDEEMING INCARNATION

Instructed about Divine essence and attributes, Saint Faustina learned that the Divine **Mercy** is the greatest of all - after (1) Holiness and (2) Justice,

> And I understood that the greatest attribute is love and mercy. It unites the creature with the Creator. This immense love and abyss of mercy are made known in the Incarnation of the Word and in the Redemption [of humanity], and it is here that I saw this as the greatest of all God's attributes (D. 180).

> God will descend to earth; the Immortal Lord of lords will abase Himself. ... The Word becomes flesh; God dwells among us, the Word of God, Mercy Incarnate. By Your descent, You have lifted us up to Your divinity.

---

[53] In *Liturgy of the Hours*, January 21, Morning Prayer, Antiphon 2.

Such is the excess of Your love, the abyss of Your mercy. Heaven is amazed at the superabundance of Your love (D. 1745).

The Angels assist in the Mystery of mysteries with their service as messengers, but God Himself is the One who executes the Mystery, the Mystery of

... God's incomprehensible love for people. He lifts us up to His very Godhead. His only motives are love and fathomless mercy. Though You make known the mystery to us through an angel, You Yourself carry it out (D. 1172).

This truth is clear: we observe the incomprehensibility of the mystery of God's essence, of His mercy, and of His truth and beauty; at the same time, God reveals Himself incomprehensible in His preferential love for a lower creature, the human being.

Saint Faustina exclaims:

O inconceivable goodness of God, ... may Your mercy be praised without cease. That You become a brother to humans, not to angels, is a miracle of the unfathomable mystery of Your mercy (D. 1584).

God assumed human nature, and by this action, truly became one with men. Having the same nature as man permitted God to have the most intimate union possible for Himself, the Creator, with a creature.

Here lies the reason for the greatness of Our Lady as the Mother of God. God, in His humility, went down to the Blessed Mary and made her His mother. To point out Mary's role, Saint Faustina compared her to the Angels, particularly to the Seraphim. Among all heavenly and earthly creatures Mary, the humble and poor of Nazareth, was chosen to become the greatest singer of the mercy of God in the history of salvation.

> The Blessed Virgin, that Snow-White Lily,
> Is first to praise the omnipotence of Your mercy.
> Her pure heart opens for the coming of the Word;
> She believes the words of God's messenger and is confirmed in trust. ...
>
> O mystery of God's mercy, O God of compassion,
> That You have deigned to leave the heavenly throne
> And to stoop down to our misery, to human weakness,
> For it is not the angels, but man who needs mercy. ...
>
> To give worthy praise to the Lord's mercy,
> We unite ourselves with Your Immaculate Mother,
> For then our hymn will be more pleasing to You,
> Because She is chosen from among men and angels (D. 1746).

The apostles and the Church teach this magnificent truth, and emphasize how much this divine humility goes far beyond any expectations of the creatures, and how it is "new, unexpected and humanly speaking incredible"[54]. The Divine Son takes on the human nature that the human beings become sons of God![55] The "greater mercy" is the justification of sinners, the forgiveness of sins.

> Justification is *the most excellent work of God's love* made manifest in Christ Jesus and granted by the Holy Spirit. It is the opinion of St. Augustine that "the justification of the wicked is a greater work than the creation of heaven and earth," because "heaven and earth will pass away but the salvation and justification of the elect ... will not pass away." (St. Augustine, *In Jo. ev.*, 72,3) He holds also that the justification of sinners surpasses the creation of the angels in justice, in that it bears witness to a greater mercy.[56]

4.1.2 "THE ANGELS WERE AMAZED"

The Infinite, Perfect God wished to assume the finite and imperfect state of a creature. For Him, this intimate union with an Angel seems unfitting. The Angel cannot comprehend this mystery because he does not possess a union with anyone

---

[54] J. RATZINGER - BENEDICT XVI, Jesus of Nazareth. *The Infancy Narratives*, Image, New York, NY 2012, 41.

[55] Cf. *Gal* 4:4-7; CCC 460.

[56] CCC 1994; cf. St. THOMAS AQ., *Summa Theologiae*, p. I, q. 21, a. 4.

of the same nature.[57] Nevertheless, God could have asked the Angels what he asked the laborers of the first hour in the parable: "Am I not allowed to do what I choose with what belongs to me?"[58]

In their test[59], some of the Angels submitted themselves to God, His plan and "His reign" in an act of renunciation (of understanding) and surrender (of the will) which we call *adoration*. Adoration is an act of rational and limited creatures before their infinitely greater Creator. The holy Angels understood that He is greater, "the Creator and Savior, the Lord and Master of everything that exists, as infinite and merciful Love" (CCC 2096). He merits the "absolute submission" (CCC 2097) from the creatures, that is adoration. They understood similarly that He, "Christ is the center of the angelic world. They are his Angels ... because they were created *through* and *for* him" (CCC 331). Therefore, in this act of submission and adoration, an act marked by *love* and *confidence*, is included any plan of God in a manner that some accepted it, while others rejected it "radically and irrevocably" (CCC 392).

The fact that God decided to manifest His glory, wisdom and especially His mercy, through the act of creation, is something extraordinary: at the end, "calling us forth from nothingness to existence" (D. 949). The same must be said of the act of not only creating man, but also sustaining

---

[57] Cf. St. THOMAS AQ., *Summa Theologiae*, p. I, q. 50, a. 4.
[58] Mt 20:15; cf. Is 55:8-10; Jr 18:1-12; Rom 11:33-35.
[59] Cf. above, ch. 2.3.

and helping him in his existence, and especially directing Himself toward the human being with His care and compassion.

However, still more admirable is the fact that God desired to empty Himself (cf. *Phil* 2:6-8), to hide His majesty and submit Himself to the fragility (exception only sin), incarnating Himself in the immaculate womb of Mary to save the world. The faithful angelic spirits followed Him, full of surprise in the face of so much mercy and humility, with total dedication, love, and disposition to serve Him in His reign.

We find various affirmations of the angels' amazement in the *Diary*:

> Heaven is amazed at the superabundance of Your love (D. 1745).

> Heaven is astounded that God has become man,
> That there is on earth a heart worthy of God Himself.
> Why is it that You do not united Yourself with a Seraph, but with a sinner, O Lord?
> Oh, because, despite the purity of the virginal womb, this is a mystery of Your mercy (D. 1746).

> And the angels were amazed at the greatness of the mercy which You have shown for mankind (D. 1743).

The Church teaches that the Son of God was accompanied by Angels in all His life on earth. Their admiration became action: "From the Incarnation to the Ascension, the life of the Word incarnate is surrounded by the adoration and service of Angels."[60]

4.2 THE INTIMACY OF GOD WITH MEN THROUGH THE EUCHARIST

With time and the increasing intimacy with her Divine spouse, Saint Faustina accepted the Will of God ever deeper and cooperated with it more intimately. She cooperated especially with God's love.

Different moments in this new period of God's saving plan involving man and the world, that is of the "economy of salvation" (CCC 489), contributed to Saint Faustina's sense of having surpassed the Angels in their love for God and was even closer to God Himself than the Seraphim are!

The Incarnation finds its continuation in the presence of God made man in the most Holy **Eucharist**. Through this Sacrament, the Divine Lover reaches all men. Saint Faustina exclaims with joy over the "Blessed Host, enchantment of all heaven" (D. 159), in this way:

I bow down before You, O Bread of Angels,

---

[60] CCC 333. The Liturgy on "the Ascension of the Lord" affirms that "the King of glory ... ascended to the highest heavens, as the Angels gazed in wonder" (ROMAN MISSAL, "Preface I of the Ascension of the Lord"). As if it were not sufficient to have decided to incarnate, suffer and die – the Son of God desired to be eternally united to the human nature.

With deep faith, hope and love ... (D. 1324; cf. D. 1350).

> Jesus, delight of my soul, Bread of Angels,
> My whole being is plunged in You,
> And I live Your divine life as do the elect in heaven ...[61].

In the description of her preparation for the encounter with Jesus in Holy Communion, at the end of her *Diary*, she offers a look at the Angels:

> Today, I am preparing myself for Your coming as a bride does for the coming of her bridegroom. He is a great Lord, this Bridegroom of mine. The heavens cannot contain Him. The Seraphim who stand closest to Him cover their faces and repeat unceasingly: Holy, Holy, Holy (D. 1805).

The incomprehensibility of God's love allowed the Saint once more to express her surprise and admiration.

> Today Jesus came to live in my heart, ...
> And He came to me in the form of bread.
>
> O Eternal God, in my bosom enclosed,
> Possessing You, I possess all Heaven,
> And with the Angels I sing to You: Holy,
> I live for Your glory alone.

---

[61] D. 1393. The expression "Bread of Angels" is found in *Psalm* 78[77]:25 and *Wis* 16:20ff; it is counted among the names for "Holy Communion" in the *Catechism* (cf. CCC 1331).

Not with a Seraph, do You unite Yourself, O God,
But with a wretched man
Who can do nothing without You;
But to him You are ever merciful.⁶²

On another occasion she expresses herself in this way:

Today, I invite Jesus to my heart, as Love. You are Love itself. All heaven catches the flame from You and is filled with love (D. 1808).

And in a hymn to the hidden Jesus in the Eucharist she prayed:

Hidden Jesus, life of my soul,
Object of my ardent desire, ...

It is You, O Host, who empower me to love forever,
And I know that You will love me as Your child in return. ...

---

⁶² D. 1231; cf. D. 522. The Church became through the Fathers of the Council in the meantime very sensitive to what the Saint described: "In the earthly liturgy we share in a foretaste of that heavenly liturgy which is celebrated in the Holy City of Jerusalem toward which we journey as pilgrims, where Christ is sitting at the right hand of God, Minister of the sanctuary and of the true tabernacle. With all the warriors of the heavenly army we sing a hymn of glory to the Lord; venerating the memory of the saints, we hope for some part and fellowship with them; we eagerly await the Savior, our Lord Jesus Christ, until He, our life, shall appear and we too will appear with Him in glory" (Vatican II, *Sacrosanctum Concilium*, 8; CCC 1090).

> Hidden Jesus, sole desire of my soul,
> You alone are to me more than the delights of heaven (D. 1427).

Saint Faustina recalls the deep respect of the Angels before their God Who made Himself so small.

> Today, I prepare for the Coming of the King. What am I, and who are You, O Lord, King of eternal glory? O my heart, are you aware of [W]ho is coming to you today? Yes, I know, ... He is the King of kings, the Lord of lords. Before Him, all power and dominion tremble. He is coming to my heart today. ... [Jesus] reassures her, saying, **See, I have left My heavenly throne to become united with you ... I want to tell you that eternal life must begin already here on earth through Holy Communion** (D. 1810, 1811).

The trembling attitude of the Angels influenced the Saint so effectively that she never forgot: in the consecrated Host is her Lord and Divine spouse truly present. Therefore, she made the effort to receive her Lord in the worthiest manner.

> I receive Holy Communion in the manner of the angels so to speak. My soul is filled with God's light and nourishes itself from Him.[63]

---

[63] D. 1278. The Little Flower has a similar idea. She writes: "I picture my soul as a patch of bare ground and I beg the Blessed Virgin to clear it of all rubbish (my imperfections) and then build there a vast pavilion fit for heaven and adorn it with her own jewels. Then I invite all the angels and saints to

4.3 CONSECRATION OF HUMAN LIFE TO CHRIST

Saint John Paul II, a great devotee of the saint from Poland, explained at the end of his Petrine Ministry how much the Church is formed by the Eucharistic Lord: "The Church draws her life from the Eucharist"; "For the most holy Eucharist contains the Church's entire spiritual wealth: Christ himself."[64] God Himself forms that community called "Church" through His Eucharistic donation.

For this reason, God not only invited Saint Faustina to Holy Communion, but He also asked that she surrender all her life to Him (cf. D. 7 - 14).

> "What more do I ask than that you give yourself entirely to Me? I care not for anything else you may give Me, for I seek not your gift but you. Just as it would not be enough for you to have everything if you did not have Me, so whatever you give cannot please Me if you do not give yourself.
>
> Offer yourself to Me, therefore, and give yourself entirely for God – your offering will be accepted. Behold, I offered Myself wholly to the Father for you, I even gave My whole Body

---

come and sing hymns of love. It seems to me that Jesus is pleased..." (St. THÉRÈSE DE LISEUX, *The Story of a Soul*, ch. VIII, Image Books, New York, NY 1989, 106).

[64] St. JOHN PAUL II, *Ecclesia de Eucharistia*, 2003, 1.

and Blood for food that I might be all yours, and you Mine forever."⁶⁵

As Christ Himself consecrates the Bread in order to give Himself to the Saint, so He desires that she may also offer her life to be consecrated and given to Him. The Church understands the religious consecration in the context of the Eucharistic Consecration, which stands at the center of Christian life, at the center of the life of the Church, and of every vocation.

> In the Eucharist, Jesus joins us to himself in his very paschal offering to the Father. We offer and are offered. Religious consecration itself assumes a Eucharistic structure, it is the total offering of self closely joined to the Eucharistic Sacrifice.⁶⁶

Already in Saint Faustina's time, before the liturgical reform, the religious profession was celebrated in the Holy Mass. Its culmination was the encounter with Jesus in Holy Communion, and all in the presence of the Angels.

So, Saint Faustina wrote first during her retreat of preparation:

> O my eternal Lord and Creator, how am I going to thank You for this great favor; namely, that You have deigned to choose miserable me

---

⁶⁵ THOMAS A KEMPIS, *Imitation of Christ*, IV, 8.
⁶⁶ CONGREGATION FOR INSTITUTES OF CONSECRATED LIFE AND SOCIETIES OF APOSTOLIC LIFE, *Starting Afresh from Christ. A Renewed Commitment to Consecrated Life in the Third Millennium*, 2002, 26.

to be Your betrothed and that You are to unite me to Yourself in an eternal bond? O dearest Treasure of my heart, I offer You all the adoration and thanksgiving of the Saints and of all the choirs of Angels, and I unite myself in a special way with Your Mother.[67]

Then the night before, she invoked "Heaven and earth", as she also did later on the occasion of the renewal of her vows (cf. D. 1369):

O Jesus, tomorrow morning I am to make my perpetual vows. I had asked heaven and earth and had called upon all beings to thank God for this immense and inconceivable favor of His when suddenly I heard these words, **My daughter, your heart is My heaven. ...** I thought: "What is it going to be like in heaven, if already here in exile God so fills my soul?" (D. 238).

Finally, during the Holy Mass:

[t]he words of Jesus during my perpetual vows: **My spouse, our hearts are joined forever. Remember to Whom you have vowed** (D. 239).

And in her answer she prayed:

Thank You, O my dearest Bridegroom, for the dignity You have conferred on me, and in

---

[67] D. 220; this sensitivity for the Divine holiness and human poverty reminds us of Saint Louis de Montfort's explanation of the "Manner of Practicing This Devotion When We Go to Holy Communion" (cf. *True Devotion to Mary*, 266-273).

particular for the royal coat-of-arms which will adorn me from this day on and which even the Angels do not possess; namely the cross, the sword, and the crown of thorns. But above all, O my Jesus, I thank You for Your Heart - it is all I need (D. 240).

In this observation, we can see the concentration on the religious consecration in Christ crucified and offered, in the God made man for the redemption of men. The consecrated virgins share in the life of their Spouse and in His mission. In this exchange, the Angels remain both amazed and distant, and these virgins become like "earthly angels," present in the life of Jesus.[68]

---

[68] Today bring to Me the meek and the humble souls and the souls of little children, and immerse them in My mercy. These souls most closely resemble My Heart. They strengthened Me during My bitter agony. I saw them as earthly Angels, who would keep vigil at My altars. I pour out upon them whole torrents of grace. Only the humble soul is able to receive My grace. I favor humble souls with My confidence (D. 1220; cf. D. 534-535).

"It is the Spirit who awakens the desire to respond fully; ... it is he who shapes and moulds the hearts of those who are called, configuring them to Christ, the chaste, poor and obedient One, ... The consecrated life thus becomes a particularly profound expression of the Church as the Bride who, prompted by the Spirit to imitate her Spouse, stands before him 'in splendour, without spot or wrinkle or any such thing, that she might be holy and without blemish' (*Eph* 5:27) ... To the degree that consecrated persons let themselves be guided by the Spirit to the heights of perfection they can exclaim: 'I see the beauty of your grace, I contemplate its radiance, I reflect its light; I am caught up in its ineffable

It is fitting, in this context, to refer to another vision of the saint on the day of the renewal of the vows of some Sisters. Saint Faustina saw Jesus and the Angels: Jesus with the sword and the Angels with the donation of the Sisters. Jesus placed the sword on one side of the scale.

It fell heavily towards the ground until it was about to touch it. Just then, the sisters finished renewing their vows. Then I saw Angels who took something from each of the sisters and placed it in a golden vessel ... on the other side of the scale, it immediately out weighed and raised up the side on which the sword had been laid. At that moment, a flame issued forth from the thurible, and it reached all the way to the brilliance. Then I heard a voice coming from the brilliance: **Put the sword back in its place; the sacrifice is greater.** Then Jesus gave us His blessing, and all I had seen vanished (D. 394).

In God's eyes, what value have love and the donation of souls to Him! God left no doubt: "I desire steadfast love and not sacrifice"[69], because the offer of oneself through obedience "is better than sacrifice" (*1Sam* 15:22).

---

splendour; I am taken outside myself as I think of myself; I see how I was and what I have become. O wonder!'" (St. JOHN PAUL II, *On The Consecrated Life and its Mission in the Church and in the World*, 1996, 19 e 20). The monks are also called *"angels of God on earth"* (ibid., 27).
[69] *Hos* 6:6; cf. Mt 9:13; Mk 12:31.

Four years later, Faustina composed a poem about the virgins. In the poem she said:

> O virgin, no one will sing your hymn.
> In your song lies hidden the love of God.
> Even the Angels do not comprehend
> What the virgins sing to God. ...
>
> O virgin, earthly angel,
> Your greatness is renowned throughout the Church.
> You stand guard before the tabernacle
> And, like a Seraph, become all love (D. 1735).

The Angels' admiration follows the Son of God incarnate, then "sacramented" in the Eucharist, and now united to the souls consecrated in His Mystical Body.

> Jesus gave me to know ... **In convents too, there are souls that fill My Heart with joy. They bear My features; therefore the Heavenly Father looks upon them with special pleasure. They will be a marvel to Angels and men. Their number is very small. They are a defense for the world before the justice of the Heavenly Father and a means of obtaining mercy for the world.**[70]

---

[70] D. 367; cf. D. 180. Pope Benedict XVI made a similar statement when he underlined the value of one single soul united with God; he applies to them the words of Pseudo-Rufinus: "The human race lives thanks to a few; were it not for them, the world would perish ..." (BENEDICT XVI, Encyclical *Spe salvi - on Christian Hope*, 2007, 15). "The prayers of one loving soul prevail more with God, both for

The love of God is also demanding. Reflecting about chastity, on this tremendous gift of Divine Mercy, Faustina heard Jesus saying these words:

You are My spouse forever; your chastity should be greater than that of the angels, for I call no angel to such intimacy as I do you. The smallest act of My spouse is of infinite value. A pure soul has inconceivable power before God (D. 534).

The Divine love in these words does not permit any soul's discouragement. In hours of discouragement, Saint Faustina recalled the Angels, and sought refuge in them. The closer the Angels are to God, the more zealously they attract souls.

Jesus, when I myself cannot sing You the hymn of love, I admire the singing of the Seraphim, they who are so dearly loved by You. I desire to drown myself in You as they do (D. 195).

And like a Seraph I repeat, "Hosanna!" ...
And for me, You surpass the delights of heaven (D. 1718; cf. D. 1393);

The Saint means this so much so that, at the end, she can say.

... I am inflamed with love by loving,
And like a Seraph I love God, though I am but weakness (D. 995).

---

the living and the dead, than the prayers of a thousand souls who love less" (St. GERTRUD THE GREAT, *Life and Revelations*, part 4, ch. 54, TAN, Rockford, IL 2002, 442).

> I will not stop singing my song of love until the choir of Angels picks it up. There is no power that can stop me in my flight toward God. I see that even the superiors do not always understand the road along which God is leading me, and I am not surprised at this (D. 761).

Even though she possessed such an intimate love of God, Saint Faustina recognized her own fragility, and therefore depended on the support, the help and company of the Holy Angels.[71]

4.4 AN EXCLUSIVE SECRET

It is evident what great value the Eucharistic Communion had for Saint Faustina:

> The most solemn moment of my life is the moment when I receive Holy Communion. I long for each Holy Communion, and for every Holy Communion I give thanks to the Most Holy Trinity (D. 1804).

At the end of her *Diary*, Saint Faustina's words lead to a still greater profundity, to one more "indwelling" in her soul, to the most intimate secret:

---

[71] We find a similar desire in other souls who love God: "If only I could be a Seraphim, to offer Him his burning ardor! ... If only I possessed the purity of the Angels to shelter Him!" (Concepción Cabrera de Armida, generally known as Conchita, in: Juan GUTIÉRREZ GONZÁLEZ, *Irresistibly Drawn to the Eucharist*, Alba House, New York, NY 2002, 13).

> I have been aware, for a long time, that Holy Communion continues in me until the next Communion. ... A vivid and even physically felt presence of God continues throughout the day and does not in the least interfere with my duties.[72]

For the reparation due to God, she confided in her Jesus, asking Him to care that she might be worthily prepared for this encounter with Him. She implored Him for an ever more intense and subtle purification:

> O my Master, shape my soul according to Your will and Your eternal designs! (D. 195; cf. D. 420).

In this mystery, Saint Faustina's vocation and mission developed, and her union with God deepened even more. In a passage about the adoration of her "*Creator and Lord, hidden in the Most Blessed Sacrament*", she confessed:

> What I talk to You about, Jesus, is our secret, which creatures shall not know and Angels dare not ask about. These are secret acts of forgiveness, known only to Jesus and me; this is the mystery of His mercy, which embraces each soul separately (D. 1692).

Another time she put it in these terms:

---

[72] D. 1821. This grace is known from other Saints as well, for ex. St. Anthony Mary Claret (*Autobiography*, Rockford IL, 1985, p. 3, ch. 18; page 180) or Bl. DINA BÉLANGER (*Autobiography*, ch. 24, on June 21, 1925).

There is one mystery which unites me with the Lord, of which no one – not even angels - may know. And even if I wanted to tell of it, I would not know how to express it. And yet, I live by it and will live by it for ever. This mystery distinguishes me from every other soul here on earth or in eternity (D. 824).

God's passion for human beings was expressed to Saint Faustina as she recorded these words in her *Diary*.

My daughter, your look disarms My anger. Although your lips are silent, you call out to Me so mightily that all heaven is moved.[73]

This affirmation requires two commentaries, one about the fact, and another about its value.

---

[73] D. 1722. God loves man so much that the entire history of salvation revolves around him. God's love is expressed especially in the mystery of the Incarnation and Eucharistic Communion. On various occasions, the Saint would speak of a preference that God gave to man before an Angel. And even before the Divine Justice, the love of souls seems to have great power. Saint Faustina once heard these words. Such intimacy reminds us for example about Moses on the mountain (cf. *Dt* 9:7-29), or about Saint Paul as St. John of the Cross explains (cf. *Spiritual Canticle*, 4, 9). It could be recalled too, that the Church calls today all to seek God in this most personal way: "I want to see God", CCC 2548-2550; CONGREGATION FOR INSTITUTES OF CONSECRATED LIFE, *Starting Afresh from Christ*, 2002, Introduction: "*Contemplating the Splendour of the Face of Christ*"; St. JOHN PAUL II, *Apostolic Letter 'On the Rosary of the Virgin Mary'*, 2002, especially 9-10; CONGREGATION FOR THE CLERGY, *Eucharistic Adoration for the Sanctification of Priests and Spiritual Maternity*, 2007).

First according to an old tradition and the constant teaching of Theology, there exists a secret between the soul and God, a secret which is even hidden before the Angels.

He who has an ear, let him hear what the Spirit says to the churches. To him who conquers I will give some of the hidden manna, and I will give him a white stone, with a new name written on the stone which no one knows except him who receives it (*Rev* 2:17).

Earlier, we find the Psalmist praying in these words, "Let the words of my mouth and the meditation of my heart be acceptable in thy sight, O Lord" (*Ps* 19[18]:14); "for thou, thou only, knowest the hearts of the children of men" (*2Cron* 6:30; cf. *1Kings* 8:39), You know "the secrets of the heart"[74].

St. Thomas explains it in this way: "Angels are never enlightened by men concerning Divine things. But men can by means of speech make known to Angels the thoughts of their hearts since it belongs to God alone to know the heart's secrets."[75] Father John Hardon responds to the question "whether Angels know secret thoughts. In one word, the answer is, 'no.' What is proper to

---

[74] *Ps* 44:21; cf. *Prov* 16:2; *Jer* 17:9-10; *1Cor* 2:11; St. THOMAS AQ., *Summa Theologiae*, p. I, q. 57, a. 4; q. 107, a. 1 ad 1; q. 114, a. 2 ad 2; q. 117, a. 2c; St. JOHN OF THE CROSS, *The Dark Night*, II, 23.1-14.

[75] St. THOMAS AQ., *Summa Theologiae*, p. I, q. 117, a. 2c.

God does not belong to Angels. It is proper only to God to read the secrets of hearts."[76]

Then, secondly, there is "the law of love" which explains the silent love as more powerful. The more two persons love each other, the less they talk, the deeper they understand each other through this love, and the smallest desire of the beloved has greater value and obliges the lover more than the greatest offer of an unknown person. Saint John of the Cross discussed this and arrived at this conclusion. When a soul arrives at this stage of union of love:

> she should not become involved in other works and exterior exercises that might be of the slightest hindrance to the attentiveness of love toward God, even though the work be of great service to God. For a little of this pure love is more precious to God and the soul and more beneficial to the Church, even if it seems one is doing nothing, than all these other works put together.[77]

Was it not so with Jesus on the Cross, being exteriorly totally passive and losing all things in the eyes of men? He gained the entire world with His eyes fixed on the Father and the few words: "Father, into thy hands I commit my spirit!" (*Lk*

---

[76] John A. HARDON, *Meditations on the Angels*, Eternal Life, Bardstown, Ky 2006, 144. It is interesting, however, to note the fact which we will still see further down: Faustina "*saw many ugly monsters. So I mentally made the sign of the cross and they disappeared immediately*" (D. 540).

[77] St. JOHN OF THE CROSS, *Spiritual Canticle*, 29.2; cf. D. 439.

23:46) and these words He pronounced almost just for our sake.

This intimacy, even hidden before the Angels, explains other affirmations of Saint Faustina which could be considered exaggerated; however, they find their explanation in this context:

> Pure love has made me strong and brave.
> I fear neither the seraphim nor the cherubim, standing with sword in hand,
> And I pass over with ease where others tremble,
> Because there is nothing to fear, there where love is the guide (D. 1632).

Before she said this, she described in careful, yet courageous steps, that she knew "Whom pure spirits adore, day and night, and for whom the hearts of the Seraphim burn with the fire of purest love" (D. 334). Besides this, she dared to compare herself to them and even desired "to surpass them in my love for"[78] Jesus. She was aware of what she said, for she asked pardon: "I apologize to you, O pure spirits, for my boldness in comparing myself to you" (D. 334).

Saint Faustina recognized the love of God for men: He loves man not because of man's greatness, not because of his strength, not because of

---

[78] D. 334. Saint Faustina does not only admire the Angels, does not only want their help in order to love God more, she wants to surpass them! Once more she says: "O Love, O queen! Love knows no fear. It passes through all the choirs of angels that stand on guard before His throne" (D. 781).

his success, but precisely because of pure divine mercy.

> I, this chasm of misery, this abyss of misery; and You, O God, who are the incomprehensible abyss of mercy, swallow me up as the heat of the sun swallows up a drop of dew! A loving look from You will fill up any abyss (D. 334).

After these observations we understand the following hymn about the Eucharistic Jesus:

> To stay at Your feet, O hidden God,
> Is the delight and paradise of my soul. ...
> Silent conversation, alone with You,
> Is to experience what heavenly beings enjoy[79],
> ...
>
> Love and sweetness are my soul's life,
> And Your unceasing presence in my soul.
> I live on earth in constant rapture,
> And like a Seraph I repeat, "Hosanna!"
>
> O You Who are hidden, body, soul and divinity,
> Under the fragile form of bread,
> You are my life from Whom springs an abundance of graces;
> And for me, You surpass the delights of heaven.

---

[79] The Little Flower once wrote: "Silence is the sweet language of the angels and all the elect. It must also be the lot of souls who love each other in Jesus" (St. THÉRÈSE DE LISEUX, *The Poetry of Saint Therese of Liseux*, Supplementary Poem, P 7, Washington, DC 1996, 232).

> When You unite Yourself with me in Communion, O God,
> I then feel my unspeakable greatness,
> A greatness which flows from You, O Lord, I humbly confess,
> And despite my misery, with Your help, I can become a saint (D. 1718).

In the Litany of the Divine Mercy it is, therefore, well said:

> Divine Mercy, better than the heavens, ... astonishment for Angels, incomprehensible to Saints, I trust in You (D. 949).

Taking in consideration the course made in this chapter, the four steps of the incomprehensible mercy of God towards men – the Incarnation, Eucharist, religious Consecration and the personal intimacy with the Lord – are the interior way of Saint Faustina. She passes the Angels, like Mary Magdalene on the day of the resurrection of the Lord, out of greater love for Him. The Angels remained, out of respect before their Lord and God, a certain distance away.[80]

Our Saint draws this surprising conclusion.

> Hidden Jesus, Eternal Love, our Source of Life ... [b]efore creating heaven and earth, You carried us in the depths of Your Heart. ... I do not envy the Seraphim their fire, for I have a greater gift deposited in my heart. They admire You in rapture, but Your Blood mingles with

---

[80] Cf. *Jn* 20:11-14; St. JOHN OF THE CROSS, *The Dark Night*, II, 19.2.

mine. Love is heaven given us already here on earth. Oh, why do You hide in faith? Love tears away the veil (D. 278).

And still more:

I am immensely happy, although I am the least of all; and I would not change anything of what God has given me. I would not want to change places even with a Seraph, as regard the interior knowledge of God which He Himself has given me. The intimate knowledge I have of the Lord is such as no creature can comprehend, particularly, the depth of His mercy that envelops me. I am happy with everything You give me! (D. 1049).

O eternal God, how ardently I desire to glorify this greatest of Your attributes; namely, Your unfathomable mercy. I see all my littleness, and cannot compare myself to the heavenly beings who praise the Lord's mercy with holy admiration. But I, too, have found a way to give perfect glory to the incomprehensible mercy of God (D. 835).

If this were not yet sufficient, the Saint observed that she not only doesn't envy the Angels, but – if it were it possible – the Angels are the ones who would envy men!

If the angels were capable of envy, they would envy us for two things: one is the receiving of Holy Communion, and the other is suffering (D. 1804).

And once she explains what she referred to:

My Jesus, You know what my soul goes through at the recollection of these sufferings. I have often marveled that the angels and saints hold their peace at the sight of a soul suffering like that. Yet they have special love for us at such moments (D. 116).

Saint Faustina is not the first who thinks in this way. We may mention one other Saint with such thoughts, the Doctor of the Church, Saint Therese of the Divine Child. Among "her last conversations" are: "The Angels can't suffer; therefore, they are not as fortunate as I am. How astonished they would be if they suffered and felt what I feel! Yes, they'd be very surprised because so am I myself."[81]

---

[81] St. THÉRÈSE DE LISEUX, *Her Last Conversations*, (August 16.4), Washington, DC 1977, 150; in the Play "The Angels at Jesus' manger" she said, "The Angel of the Holy Face sings... Seraph, weep in silence, / You see this day-old Child. / ... Alas! Why am I an angel, / Incapable of suffering?.... / Jesus, with one sweet exchange / I would like to die for You!!!....." ("The Angels at Jesus' Manger", 25 December, 1894, in: *The Plays of Saint Thérèse of Lisieux. Pious Recreations*, Washington, DC 2008, 116). And in the same play, "The Angel of the last judgment kneels and sings ...: Before You, sweet Child, the cherubim bows [sic!] down!... / Dazed, he admires Your ineffable love. / He wishes, like You, on the somber hill / To die one day!...." Then sing "All the Angels ... How great is the good fortune of the humble creature. / The seraphim in their ecstasy would wish / To leave, O Jesus! their angelic nature / and become children!..." (Ibid., 130). – Another Doctor of the Church, Saint Francis of Sales, writes about the Holy Mass: "Hosts of Angels are always present to honor this adorable mystery,' says St. John Chrysostom (*On*

In light of this attitude is another admirable affirmation of Saint Faustina. When she asked Jesus "that all the souls who will die today escape the fire of hell," she justified her petition with these words: "The Angels will not be surprised at this," because they already conformed themselves to the fact that "Your mercy is inconceivable" (D. 873).

4.5 THE ANGELS IN ZEALOUS CLOSENESS AND RESPECTFUL DISTANCE

As did nearly all authentic mystics, Saint Faustina lived a normal tension within herself. On one side she sensed a great attraction to God, the Father, Son, and Holy Spirit, and on the other side, she simultaneously sensed pain for not being able to unite herself to Him as the heart desires (or as Jesus expects from her according to her way of seeing it). In these hours she wanted to be united with the highest Angels:

> Hidden Jesus, take at last to Yourself my thirsting heart
> Which burns for You with the pure fire of the Seraphim (D. 1427).

---

the Priesthood, VI, 4,15). If we were there with them and have the same intention, we cannot help receiving many favorable influences from this association. The choirs of the Church triumphant and those of the Church militant are united to the Lord in this divine action..." (St. FRANCIS OF SALES, *Introduction to Devote Life*, II, 14.3).

We can observe two attitudes on the side of the Angels: a great desire for union and a respectful distance.

4.5.1 THE DESIRED UNION WITH THE ANGELS

Saint Faustina desired here that her heart would burn "with the pure fire of the Sera-phim" (D. 1427). She spoke of "seraphic souls, from whom God demands greater love than He does from others" (D. 1556). The Seraphim are closest to the Throne of God as Tradition says and she mentions (cf. D. 1805). Their love is ardent;[82] God can permit that they approach one as His instruments. This love would free one from tepidity or indifference; it purifies and gives new life.

> Then flew one of the Seraphim to me, having in his hand a burning coal which he had taken with tongs from the altar. And he touched my mouth, and said: "Behold, this has touched your lips; your guilt is taken away, and your sin forgiven".[83]

---

[82] "We must therefore acknowledge, with the praise due to the creator, that not only of holy men, but also of the holy Angels, it can be said that 'the love of God is shed abroad in their hearts by the Holy Ghost, which is given unto them.' (*Rom* 5:5)" (St. AUGUSTINE, *City of God*, XII, 9.2; cf. XI, 33).

[83] *Is* 6:6-7; Pseudo-Dionysius says: "There is nothing unreasonable in the representation of the Seraph as purifying the prophet; for just as God Himself, the cause of every purification, purifies all, ... so also the Angel who purifies the prophet refers his own purifying power and knowledge to God as its origin" (*The Celestial Hierarchy*, ch. 13,4).

In the history of the Church, references have been made to the "seraphic love" of St. Francis or to the "seraphic doctor" Saint Bonaventure. Saint Margaret Mary Alacoque, the great devotee and messenger of the Sacred Heart of Jesus, wrote about the union with the Seraphim in her autobiography in the following terms:

> Another time, when the Sisters were working in common, picking hemp, I withdrew into a small courtyard, near the Blessed Sacrament, where, doing my work on my knees, I felt myself wholly rapt in interior and exterior recollection, and at the same time, the Adorable Heart of my Jesus appeared to me brighter than the sun. I was surrounded by the flames of Its pure love, and encircled by Seraphim, who sang in marvelous harmony: "Love triumphs, love enjoys, the love of the Sacred Heart rejoices!"
>
> These blessed spirits invited me to unite with them in praising this Divine Heart, but I did not dare do so. They reproved me, telling me they had come in order to form an association with me, whereby to render It a perpetual homage of love, adoration and praise, and that, for this purpose, they would take my place before the Blessed Sacrament. Thus I might be able, by their means, to love It continually, and, as they would participate in my love and suffer in my person, I, on my part, should rejoice in and with them. At the same time they wrote this association in the Sacred Heart in letters of gold, and in indelible characters of

love. ... From that day on I addressed them by no other name, when praying to them, than by that of my divine associates.[84]

Here is an intimate union with mutual exchange: The Angels allow man to participate in their perennial praise and in their adoration, and they, on the basis of the communion of love, participate in the suffering of man. "As they ... suffer in my person, I, on my part, should rejoice in and with them." Thus, God permits the holy Angels to practice the virtue of mercy with the creatures, since this is impossible among themselves. In this way they become similar to their own Creator and Lord, the Merciful.

4.5.2 THE ANGELIC RESPECTFUL DISTANCE

There exists a respectful distance between Angels and God. Saint Faustina saw how the Seraphim cover their faces and how all the power and dominion tremble before Jesus. The Angels see in the Eucharistic Jesus, first His Divinity and then His humanity. Their clear vision of God in heaven, and in the Eucharist on earth, pushes them to the highest respect before their Divine Lord and to the effort to lead all to the same holy fear before this hidden God on earth.

To illustrate this holy distance between God, Angels, and man, it is worthwhile to bring here the entire report about the "Angel of the Wrath of God." Certainly, not one Angel acts with his own

---

[84] St. MARGARET MARY, *The Autobiography*, TAN, Rockford, IL 1986, n. 101.

will. It was God Himself Who showed Saint Faustina this Angel.

The following day, Friday, September 13, 1935 (D. 473).

In the evening, when I was in my cell, I saw an Angel, the executor of divine wrath. He was clothed in a dazzling robe, his face gloriously bright, a cloud beneath his feet. From the cloud, bolts of thunder and flashes of lightning were springing into his hands; and from his hand they were going forth, and only then were they striking the earth. When I saw this sign of divine wrath which was about to strike the earth, and in particular a certain place, which for good reasons I cannot name, I began to implore the Angel to hold off for a few moments, and the world would do penance. But my plea was a mere nothing in the face of the divine anger. Just then I saw the Most Holy Trinity. The greatness of Its majesty pierced me deeply, and I did not dare to repeat my entreaties. At that very moment I felt in my soul the power of Jesus' grace, which dwells in my soul. When I became conscious of this grace, I was instantly snatched up before the Throne of God. Oh, how great is our Lord and God and how incomprehensible His holiness! I will make no attempt to describe this greatness, because before long we shall all see Him as He is. I found myself pleading with God for the world with words heard interiorly.

As I was praying in this manner, I saw the Angel's helplessness; he could not carry out the just punishment which was rightly due for sins. Never before had I prayed with such inner power as I did then (D. 474).

This report is composed of different points which need to be distinguished:

1 – The Angel, the executor, makes a strong impression; he appears and was about to touch the earth. Saint Faustina wanted to make him stop, and began to pray to the Angel, but her prayer did not have any power.

2 – When she was absorbed in God, she did not even want to pray anymore. She had sensed the grace of Jesus in her and was snatched up before the Throne of God. Then she prayed with words which did not come from her, but which she heard interiorly.

3 – And "praying in this manner. I saw the Angel's helplessness" to "carry out the just punishment."

We can observe a similar development as described in the famous third secret of Fatima, revealed to Lucy on July 13 of 1917:

1 – An "Angel with a flaming sword ... flashing, it gave out flames that looked as though they would set the world on fire."

2 – "But they died out in contact with the splendor that Our Lady radiated towards him." And pointing to the earth with his right hand, the Angel cried out in a loud voice: "Penance, penance, penance!" followed by the terrible vision of the bloody persecution of the Church.

3 - At the end "there were two Angels" gathering "up the blood of the Martyrs and with it sprinkled the souls that were making their way to God".

To turn an Angel away from his mission, and even to turn the wrath of God away from its execution, is not easy. When God sent an Angel before Israel, He asked: "Give heed to him, and hearken to his voice ... he will not pardon your transgression, for my name is in him" (Ex 23:21). The Angel does not act by himself; therefore, it does not help to negotiate with him, as was the first reaction of Saint Faustina: "I began to implore the Angel ... But my plea was a mere nothing" (D. 474). What was it then that made the Angel stop? Was it just more effort on her part than before, as she said at the end: "Never before had I prayed with such inner power as I did then" (D. 474); or was it the words she heard interiorly that made the difference?

By divine inspiration, Sister Faustina had recourse to *the merits of the Passion of the Son of God* which have an infinite value.

> The words with which I entreated God are these: **Eternal Father, I offer You the Body and Blood, Soul and Divinity of Your dearly beloved Son, Our Lord Jesus Christ for our sins and those of the whole world; for the sake of His sorrowful Passion, have mercy on us** (D. 475).

Consequently, it was not effort on the part of the Saint, but rather the recourse to the Son of

God incarnated. Through an interior impulse she offered to the Father His own eternal Son: His "Body and Blood, Soul and Divinity" and "His sorrowful passion". The strength of the eternal Divine Son made man before His eternal Father, made the Angel helpless and incapable of his mission: "I saw the Angel's helplessness; he could not carry out the just punishment," the Angel, "the executor of divine wrath"[85]!

This reveals also the secret of the spouse of Jesus; we had already heard her saying: "Your Blood mingles with mine. Love is heaven given us already here on earth" (D. 278).

It is particular to the Eucharistic Jesus Himself with His Blood to transform the soul in such a way that it remains united with Him and is able to please and love the Eternal Father.

Saint Paul explained this when he spoke about Christian marriage. It is necessary to start with the love of Christ for the Church and then to imitate His love. He said:

> "Husbands, love your wives, as Christ loved the Church and gave himself up for her, that he might sanctify her, having cleansed her by the washing of water with the word, that he might

---

[85] D. 474. **"This prayer will serve to appease My wrath"** (D. 476) said Jesus. It surprises us that this invocation, on one occasion offered for an afflicted person, was more effective than the presence of an Angel (cf. D. 1565). We find in the *Diary* various references about the immense value of the merits of the Passion of Christ (cf. e.g. D. 367-369).

present the church to himself in splendor, without spot or wrinkle or any such thing, that she might be holy and without blemish" (*Eph* 5:25-27).

Therefore, the cause of the familiarity of the spouse with the Divine spouse is also the cause of the helplessness of the Angel of the Divine Wrath or the cause of the reconciliation of men with God. Thus, Saint Paul notes in another place: "In Him (Christ) all the fullness of God was pleased to dwell, and through Him reconcile to Himself all things, whether on earth or in heaven, making peace by the blood of His cross" (*Col* 1:19-20), the cross that "fashioned men into Angels"[86].

This is the secret of the Church and the souls in her, the secret of the mystery - incomprehensible for the Angels, the mystery of the power of the Saints. God shows Saint Faustina the bond of her love for Jesus, and clinging to it, she participates in the power of the One whom the Angels obey, as in heaven so on earth, so that the Saint could write: "The devils were full of hatred for me, but they had to obey me at the command of God" (D. 741).

The Angels stand at a reverent distance to the Incarnate Son of God. It seems, according to Saint Faustina, that at the same time, they approach

---

[86] St. JOHN CHRYSOSTOM, "Homily LIV on Mt 16:13", in: Nicene and Post-Nicene Fathers, vol. 10: CHRYSOSTOM, *Homilies on the Gospel of Saint Matthew*, Hendrickson Publishers, Peabody, Mass, ²1999, 336; cf. Mike Aquilina, *A year with the Angels. Daily Meditations with the Messengers of God*, St. Benedict Press, Charlotte, NC, 2011, 194-200.

closer and closer, recognizing in man the image and presence of their Lord and God and the mysterious fruit of the life of these souls because of their union with Jesus, in particular of their sufferings which bring them closer to Jesus Crucified and Risen. The Cross and its memorial, the Eucharistic Jesus, becomes the meeting point for Angel and man, and their union is in Christ! That might have been the reason why the Church concludes the treatise on the Angels in the Catechism with these words: "Already here on earth the Christian life shares by faith in the blessed company of Angels and men united in God" (CCC 336).

5. THE HELP OF THE ANGELS

Previous chapters contain many references that open one's vision into the world of the Angels. This chapter will delve into the many forms in which the Angels did help Saint Faustina. Very naturally, she narrated the interventions the Angels offered her; Saint Faustina did not go into great accounts of the explications or justifications of the Angels' interventions. She gave various references to her prayers to the holy Angels. In this chapter, the importance of the help of the holy Angels as well as the reaction to that help by the fallen angels will be covered.

5.1 HELP OF HIGHER ANGELS

5.1.1 IN SPIRITUAL LIFE

Since the Saint never wanted to abandon her union with God, she affirmed that she never stopped praying until she was sure that the Angels would continue in her place:

> I desire very much to be united with You, but Your works hold me back. ... With you, Jesus, I go through life, amid storms and rainbows, with a cry of joy, singing the song of Your mercy. I will not stop singing my song of love until the choir of Angels picks it up (D. 761).

"In her liturgy, the Church joins with the Angels to adore the thrice-holy God. She invokes their assistance" (CCC 335). And it is principally in the Holy Mass that men and Angels are "united in God"[87]. Saint Faustina comments:

> (O)ne of the seven spirits who stand before the throne of God day and night ... during Holy Mass, before the Elevation, began to sing these words: "Holy, Holy. Holy". His voice was like that of a thousand voices; it is impossible to put it into words (D. 471).

When the Saint stayed in the hospital and remained, in the eyes of men, too weak to participate at Holy Mass and even to receive Holy Communion – a heavy cross for a loving soul as Faustina – God sent her a Seraph with the Blessed Sacrament. It is worthwhile to quote the entire record about this since it did not happen only once, but for thirteen days.

> In the evening, the sister ... who was to look after me came and said, "Tomorrow you will not receive the Lord Jesus, Sister, because you are very tired; later on, we shall see." This hurt me very much, but I said with great calmness, "Very well," and, resigning myself totally to the will of the Lord, I tried to sleep. In the morning, I made my meditation and prepared for Holy Communion, even though I was not

---

[87] CCC 336. The testimony about the presence of the Angels in the Liturgy, especially at the Holy Mass, is found in all centuries; for example in the Early Church through Saint John Chrysostom; in the Middle Age through Saint Brigit and, in our time, through Saint Padre Pio (cf. J. DANIELOU, *The Angels and Their Mission*, ch. 6, 62-66; esp. E. PETERSON, *The Book on the Angels*).

to receive the Lord Jesus. When my love and desire had reached a high degree, I saw at my bedside a Seraph, who gave me Holy Communion, saying these words: "Behold the Lord of Angels." When I received the Lord, my spirit was drowned in the love of God and in amazement. This was repeated for thirteen days, although I was never sure he would bring me Holy Communion the next day. Yet, I put my trust completely in the goodness of God, but did not even dare to think that I would receive Holy Communion in this way on the following day. ... As soon as he [the Seraph] gave me the Lord, he disappeared (D. 1676).

We also know of this experience in the life of various Saints. It is said of Saint Agnes of Montepulcan (+ 1317) that she received Holy Communion through an Angel ten times, and Saint Stanislaus Kostka (+ 1568) twice in different places.[88] This grace is known in our times in the life of Saint Gemma Galgani[89] and more so as a part of the events in Fatima: The Angel brought Holy Communion to the three little Shepherds at his last apparition to them.[90]

---

[88] Cf. F. HOLBÖCK, *Vereint mit den Engeln und Heiligen*, Christiana-Verlag, Stein am Rhein 1984, 335.

[89] Cf. Tito P. ZECCA, *Così Lontani così Vicini. Gli angeli nella vita e negli scritti di Gemma Galgani*, Paoline, Milano 1998, 162-163.

[90] Cf. *Fatima in Lucia's own Words. Sister Lucia's Memoirs*, Fatima 1998, 64-65 and 161-162.

Continuing with the impressive testimony of Saint Faustina with the experience of the limitation of the Angel in one of these thirteen visits, she mentions:

> ... when a certain doubt rose within me shortly before Holy Communion, the Seraph with the Lord Jesus stood before me again. I asked the Lord Jesus, and not receiving an answer, I said to the Seraph, "Could you perhaps hear my confession?" And he answered me, "No spirit in heaven has that power." And at that moment, the Sacred Host rested on my lips (D. 1677).

As God reserves a corner in the soul exclusively all for Himself, so, in the economy of salvation, also exists that region which God reserves for well-determined persons, like ordained priests: "Priests have received from God a power that he has given neither to Angels nor to Archangels. ... God above confirms what priests do here below" (CCC 983), affirms Saint Chrysostom. And Saint Faustina confesses:

> Jesus defends whatever the priest says, ... through a special grace, I have come to know very clearly to what extent You have shared Your power and mystery with them, more so than with the Angels (D. 1240).

The Angels cooperate with the priest, especially in the communication of graces, but they don't have the power to consecrate or absolve, acting "in the person of Christ."[91] What the Angels can do is conduct the ways of the priests and faithful in such a way that they find each other. And how many times they did this in the life of this saintly apostle of Divine Mercy!

Saint Faustina experienced another cross in her life with the Angels. The holy Angels' presence and help, especially in the interior and spiritual life, does not always calm down the soul, but stimulates it even more to seek God and, in this way, increases the anxiety, the famine, and thirst for God, the pain of love. This is how Saint Faustina describes it:

> One day, when I was at adoration, and my spirit seemed to be dying for Him, and I could no longer hold back my tears, I saw a spirit of great beauty who spoke these words to me: "Don't cry - says the Lord." ... Yet this spirit did not soothe my yearning, but roused me to even greater longing for God (D. 471).

5.1.2 IN DAILY LIFE

Saint Faustina, like all the Saints, turned to God as well as to the Angels with great simplicity and confidence. In fact, she depended on their help in all circumstances and in any need. And the Angels not only confirmed, but also justified her trust in them.

When Saint Faustina had to be at the gate of the Convent, she was afraid. She relates:

---

[91] Vatican II, *Presbyterorum Ordinis*, 2.

When I heard how dangerous it was to be at the gate these days because of revolutionary disturbances and how many evil people have a hatred for convents, I went in and had a talk with the Lord and asked Him to so arrange it that no evil person would dare come to the gate. Then I heard these words: **My daughter, the moment you went to the gate I set a Cherub over it to guard it. Be at peace** (D. 1271).

Jesus had placed a Cherub at the gate for her; so, she had to calm down. Additionally, Jesus allowed her to see the Angel,

... a Cherub with his hands joined. His gaze was like lightening, and I understood how the fire of God's love burns in that look ... (D. 1271).

On another occasion the Saint speaks about the company of one of the seven Angels who was always at her side.

Then I saw one of the seven spirits near me, radiant as at other times, under a form of light. I constantly saw him beside me when I was riding on the train (D. 630).

The Saint did not identify him as her Guardian Angel, or she at least did not affirm this. In fact, other Angels can be part of one's life, helping and interceding. They can be called *Angels-companions*, that is, Angels who are sent by God for a certain task or a special mission. Saint Petrus Canisius testified to just such a case in his mission to Germany.[92]

Saint Faustina's mission certainly was so great that, besides her Guardian Angel, a special and permanent assistance by an additional Angel was justified. "This spirit does not leave me for a single moment, but accompanies me everywhere" (D. 471).

Similar affirmations are found with regard to Saint Michael. God himself asked him to take care of our Saint in a particular way.

> On the Feast of Saint Michael the Archangel, I saw by my side that great Leader, who spoke these words to me: "The Lord has ordered me to take special care of you. Know that you are hated by evil; but do not fear – 'Who is like God!'" And he disappeared. But I feel his presence and assistance (D. 706).

It is not certain if this grace was the fruit of her special devotion to St. Michael or if it was because of a special need, related to her vocation and mission. The fact is that Saint Faustina sensed a vivid presence of this great defender and soldier of God.

The Angels communicate among themselves and then call the one who can help or serve. The beautiful actions of the Angels in the life of man show how necessary are the awareness and the willingness of man to cooperate with the Angels.

---

[92] Cf. St. PETRUS CANISIUS, *Confessions and Testament*, ch. 2 and 3.

There is a biblical example of this in the life of Daniel who received a meal through the mediation of "the Angel of the Lord" and the prophet Habakkuk (cf. *Dan* 14:33-39).

Life in communion with the Angels can be better understood when we look at the Guardian Angel in the history of Saint Faustina.

5.2 THE GUARDIAN ANGEL

5.2.1 THREE EXCEPTIONAL TRIPS

Saint Faustina had recently entered the convent, in the year 1925, when she asked the Lord: "... whom else I should pray for?"(D. 20) In answer to this prayer to Jesus, her Guardian Angel was sent: "I saw my Guardian Angel, who ordered me to follow him" (ibid.). He led her to *purgatory*,

> ... in a misty place full of fire in which there was a great crowd of suffering souls. They were praying fervently, but to no avail, for themselves; only we can come to their aid. The flames which were burning them did not touch me at all. My Guardian Angel did not leave me for an instant. I asked these souls what their greatest suffering was. They answered me in one voice that their greatest torment was longing for God. I saw Our Lady visiting the souls in Purgatory. ... She brings them refreshment. I wanted to talk with them some more, but my Guardian Angel beckoned me to leave (D. 20).

Years later, in 1936, Sister Faustina speaks about another "trip", this time to heaven, to "the throne of God".

> I suddenly saw my Guardian Angel, who led me before the throne of God. I passed through great hosts of saints. ... When they wanted to say more, my Guardian Angel beckoned me to be silent, and I came before the throne of God. I saw a great and inaccessible light. ... my Guardian Angel said to me, "Here is your throne, for your faithfulness in fulfilling the will of God" (D. 683).

Months later, Saint Faustina, accompanied by an Angel, received the grace of a visit to hell. She does not specify what Angel it was, for this reason it is not excluded that, as at the other times, it was the Guardian Angel.

> Today, I was led by an Angel to the chasms of hell. It is a place of great torture; how awesomely large and extensive it is! The kinds of tortures I saw: the first torture that constitutes hell is the loss of God; ... the fifth torture is continual darkness and a terrible suffocating smell, and, despite the darkness, the devils and the souls of the damned see each other and all the evil, both of others and their own; the sixth torture is the constant company of Satan; the seventh torture is horrible despair, hatred of God, vile words, curses and blasphemies. These are the tortures suffered by all the damned together, but that is not the end of the sufferings (D. 741).

These three "trips" bring to mind the famous "dreams" of Saint Don Bosco in the century before Saint Faustina. He saw in his room "the man of the night before," who told him: "Get up and come with me!" He led the Saint to hell and purgatory, similarly to the Guardian Angel of Saint Faustina; at his visit to heaven, Don Bosco does not mention such a guide.[93]

5.2.2　A SPECIAL MISSION AND "MYSTERIOUS UNION"

Saint Faustina discovered and realized progressively the plans of God. One of the distinct elements of her mission would be her participation in the spiritual good of the agonizing: "God has given me a wondrous contact with the dying!" (D. 835), and this together with the Guardian Angels.

Saint Faustina was not even aware that this mission was realized through the visits her Guardian Angel made. At the beginning of one of her reports she expressed herself in this way:

> My Guardian Angel told me to pray for a certain soul, and in the morning I learned that it was a man whose agony had begun that very moment (D. 820).

And then she continued saying:

---

[93] Cf. E.M. BROWN, ed., *Dreams, Visions & Prophesies of Don Bosco*, Don Bosco Publications, New Rochelle, NY 1986, 239-253.

> The Lord Jesus makes it known to me in a special way when someone is in need of my prayer (D. 820).

Sometimes she does not determine whose "spirit" it is, her Guardian Angel or the one of the dying person.

> Suddenly, I realize interiorly and am aware of who the spirit is who is asking this of me; I pray until I feel at peace (D. 834).

> I was not aware that souls are so closely united, and often it is my Guardian Angel who tells me (D. 828).

She speaks about the grace of this union of her soul with the soul of the dying person.

The fact is that the Guardian Angel of Saint Faustina participates in this work of mercy in favor of the dying.

> When I went to the garden one afternoon, my Guardian Angel said to me, "Pray for the dying." And so I began at once to pray the rosary with the gardeners for the dying. After the rosary, we said various prayers for the dying. After the prayers, the wards began to chat gayly [sic!] among themselves. In spite of the noise they were making, I heard these words in my soul: "Pray for me!" But as I could not understand these words very well, I moved a few steps away from the wards, trying to think who it could be who was asking me to pray. Then I heard the words, "I am Sister ...." This sister was in Warsaw while I was, at the

time, in Vilnius. "Pray for me until I tell you to stop. I am dying." Immediately, I began to pray fervently for her, [addressing myself] [sic!] to the expiring Heart of Jesus. She gave me no respite, and I kept praying from three [o'clock] [sic!] until five. At five I heard the words: "Thank you!" and I understood that she had died. But during Holy Mass on the following day, I continued to pray fervently for her soul. In the afternoon, a postcard came saying that Sister... had died at such and such a time. I understood that it was at the same hour when she said to me "Pray for me" (D. 314).

On another occasion, "the Lord said to me, **My daughter, help Me to save a certain dying sinner...**" And thanks to her prayer, "The sick man peacefully breathed his last" (D. 1565).

5.2.3 COMPANY, PROTECTION AND CONSOLATION

Saint Faustina relates in three moments the help of her Guardian Angel who serves as testimony of the promises of the Psalmist:

"The Angel of the Lord encamps around those who fear him, and delivers them" (*Ps* 34[33]:7).

"Let them be like chaff before the wind, with the Angel of the Lord driving them on! Let their way be dark and slippery, with the Angel of the Lord pursuing them!" (*Ps* 35[34]:5-6).

"For he will give his Angels charge of you to guard you in all your ways" (*Ps* 91[90]:11).

This Saint relates how the contemplation of nature – "I looked up from my cell to the sky and saw the beautiful star-strewn firmament and the moon" (D. 470) – awaked in her an attraction to the God Creator, "an inconceivable fire of love for my Creator welled up within my soul and, unable to bear the yearning for Him that arose within my soul" (D. 470). And when she gave in to these emotions, "I wept aloud" (D. 470). But then, her Guardian Angel touched her and said: "The Lord orders me to tell you to rise from the ground,'" (D. 470) which she did immediately, however without being consoled interiorly as she wished. "I ... felt no consolation in my soul. The yearning for God grew even stronger in me" (D. 470). It seems that the Angel did not permit these sentiments. In the name of the Lord Himself, the Angel came and asked that she might confront the cross of unsatisfied emotions.

The Guardian Angel's companionship in the ordinary steps of life is better known than the spiritual companionship he offered. Saint Faustina saw herself accompanied by her Guardian Angel on the entire trip to Warsaw and Krakow, he only disappeared "... when we arrived at the convent entrance" (D. 490).

In the New Testament the Angels are at the service of Jesus and also of the Christian community, accompanying their steps; that is the reason why the "Angel of the Lord" addressed once Philip saying: "'Rise and go toward the south to the road that goes down from Jerusalem to Gaza.' ... And he rose and went. And behold" (Acts 8:26-27), he found a rich and pious Ethiopian, ready to embrace the faith.

In a third episode, Saint Faustina tells how the Guardian Angel protected her, or how she "tread on the lion and the adder," and trampled "the serpent ... under foot" (*Ps* 91[90]:13). Saint Faustina left a ceremony in the church to return home. She described the event:

> I was in a hurry to get back home. When I had taken a few steps, a great multitude of demons blocked my way. They threatened me with terrible tortures ... Seeing their great hatred for me, I immediately asked my Guardian Angel for help, and at once the bright and radiant figure of my Guardian Angel appeared and said to me, "Do not fear, spouse of my Lord" (D. 418, 419).

Something similar happened to Tobias: having expulsed the demon, his companion, the Archangel Raphael, followed the demon who "fled to the remotest parts of Egypt," and there "the Angel bound him" (*Tb* 8:3); this way Tobias could have a peaceful life in his marriage with Sarah.

This powerful and instantaneous assistance of Angels prepares one to look at the actions of the fallen angels in the life of the Saint of Divine Mercy.

6. THE ENEMY OF THE SONS OF GOD

6.1 THE FACT OF DIABOLIC ATTACKS AND THEIR MEANING

6.1.1 THE FACT

One may be astonished to discover that the devil was active in Saint Faustina's life. One quickly realizes that she was especially hated by the fallen angels, namely because of her mission, which affected and still affects them very much.

> Suddenly, my cell was filled with black figures full of anger and hatred for me. One of them said, "Be damned, you and He who is within you, for you are beginning to torment us even in hell."[94]

> **But know, my child, that Satan hates you; ... he burns with a particular hatred for you, because you have snatched so many souls from his dominion** (D. 412).

Or on another occasion she observed:

> The Evil Spirit howled with fury. "Oh, if I had power over you!" and disappeared (D. 1465).

To understand such an amount of hate it is necessary to take into consideration two factors: Saint Faustina was Christian and consecrated. She tried to live in the state of grace and union with God. She made every effort to fulfill her vocation

---

[94] D. 323; cf. D. 40; 741; 1115; 1167.

and mission. Finally, God had chosen her as instrument of an extraordinary work in His Church. From her, a spirituality and apostolate of Divine Mercy would be begun; and the demons hate the merciful love of God for men because unlike or contrary to many sinners, the fallen angels are incapable of repenting.

> How terribly Satan hates God's mercy! I see how he opposes this whole work (D. 812).

> Satan has admitted to me that I am the object of his hatred. He said that "a thousand souls do me less harm than you do when you speak of the great mercy of the Almighty One. The greatest sinners regain confidence and return to God, and I lose everything. But what is more, you persecute me personally with that unfathomable mercy of the Almighty One." I took note of the great hatred Satan has for the Mercy of God. He does not want to acknowledge that God is good.[95]

6.1.2 THE UNIVERSAL FACT

The life of the Saint of Divine Mercy is a living testimony of the rebellion of the fallen angels and illustrates what the Fathers of the Second Vatican Council affirmed.

"This dramatic situation of 'the whole world [which] is in the power of the evil one' (*1Jn* 5:19; cf. *1Pet* 5:8) makes man's life a battle:

---

[95] D. 1167; cf. D. 741; 764; 1115; 1583; 1659.

"The whole of man's history has been the story of dour combat with the powers of evil, stretching, so our Lord tells us, from the very dawn of history until the last day. Finding himself in the midst of the battlefield man has to struggle to do what is right, and it is at great cost to himself, and aided by God's grace, that he succeeds in achieving his own inner integrity"[96]. (CCC 409)

Jesus Himself warns us of the possibility of the devil's actions. He said very frankly that He will send his disciples among wolves: "I send you out as sheep in the midst of wolves; so be wise as serpents and innocent as doves" (Mt 10:16).

In addition, both Saint Peter and Saint Paul, pillars among the apostles, alert the faithful: "Be sober, be watchful. Your adversary the devil prowls around like a roaring lion, seeking some one to devour" (*1Pet* 5:8). And Saint Paul writes to the Ephesians very determined: "We are not contending against flesh and blood, but against the principalities, against the powers, against the world rulers of this present darkness, against the spiritual hosts of wickedness in the heavenly places" (*Eph* 6:12).

Saint Faustina saw the reality of the danger that exists in our human life on earth. She wrote:

When I entered the chapel in the morning I heard a voice in my soul, **You are united to**

---

[96] Vatican II, *Gaudium et spes*, 37,2.

Me; fear nothing. But know, my child, that Satan hates you; he hates every soul (D. 412).

By an extraordinary grace of the Lord, she saw "many souls rushing headlong into the terrible abyss of hell" (D. 929).

6.1.3 THE MEANING OF FAUSTINA'S EXPERIENCE

The fact that all men have to deal with diabolic troubles is the great call to the discernment of spirits, to the "practice to distinguish good from evil"[97] and makes the experience of Saint Faustina an example of value. Jesus said explicitly through her:

The graces I grant you are not for you alone, but for a great number of other souls as well (D. 723).

To understand this well, we should give first some general rules.

(1) The Church warns about the danger to give too much attention to "diabolic activity." She gives two reasons.

First, the actions of the fallen angels are under God's control:

The power of Satan is, nonetheless, not infinite. He is only a creature, powerful from the fact that he is pure spirit, but still a creature. He cannot prevent the building up of God's reign. Although Satan may act in the world out of hatred for God and his kingdom

---

[97] *Heb* 5:14; cf. *Zech* 13:7-9; *Rom* 12:2; *1Cor* 12:10; *1Thess* 5:19f; *1Pet* 3:7; *1Jn* 4:1; *Is* 5:20; D. 29, 122, 633 etc..

in Christ Jesus, and although his action may cause grave injuries – of a spiritual nature and, indirectly, even of a physical nature – to each man and to society, the action is permitted by divine providence which with strength and gentleness guides human and cosmic history. It is a great mystery that providence should permit diabolical activity, but "we know that in everything God works for good with those who love him" (*Rom* 8:28)[98].

Saint Faustina words speak about this Divine dominion:

> The glory of the Divine Mercy is resounding, ... I have clearly seen that the will of God is already being carried out, and that it will be accomplished to the very last detail. The

---

[98] CCC 395. We may consider, as a proof of the sovereignty of God before the devils, the fact that Saint Faustina found the devil in purgatory, namely as "an instrument of penance" and as purification of the souls. Saint Faustina saw in purgatory among the souls "many demons" (D. 412), and, in fact, the Church believes in this possibility as she prays in the *Liturgy of the Hours*: "Be merciful to the faithful departed, keep them from the power of the Evil One" (*Liturgy of the Hours*, Intercessions of the Evening Prayer, on Wednesday of the 3rd Week in Ordinary Time; cf. St. THOMAS AQ., *Summa Theologiae*, *Supplementum*, Append. q. 1, a. 5). Our Saint concludes: "I know well that the wretch will not touch me without God's willing it, but what is he up to? He is beginning to attack me openly and with such great fury and hate, but he does not disturb my peace for a moment, and this composure of mine makes him furious" (D. 713).

enemy's greatest efforts will not thwart the smallest detail of what the Lord has decreed[99].

But Satan has only as much influence over the soul as God allows him, and God knows how much we can bear (D. 98).

The second reason: God gave man the glory of a free will that no devil can take, so that no person should fear being helplessly exposed to the evil powers.

Popular devotion to the Holy Angels, which is legitimate and good, can, however, also give rise to possible deviations:

when, as it can sometimes happen, the faithful are taken by the idea that the world is subject to demiurgical struggles, or an incessant battle between good and evil spirits, or Angels and demons, in which man is left at the mercy of superior forces and over which he is helpless; such cosmologies bear little relation to the true Gospel vision of the struggle to overcome the Devil, which requires moral commitment, a fundamental option for the Gospel, humility, and prayer;

when the daily events of life, which have nothing or little to do with our progressive maturing on the journey towards Christ, are

---

[99] D. 1659. This is like we read in Book of Revelation: "God has put it into their hearts to carry out His purpose by being of one mind and giving over their royal power to the beast, *until* the words of God shall be fulfilled" (*Rev* 17:17; cf. *Job* 1:12; 2:6).

read schematically or simplistically, indeed, childishly, so as to ascribe all setbacks to the Devil and all success to the Guardian Angels.[100]

(2) Not everyone must expect such bold attacks as Saint Faustina experienced. The devil, like a smart psychologist, adapts his method to the individuals. Therefore it is good to observe these fundamental rules:

- Souls who still struggle with sin – are especially attacked by seduction or through attraction to creatures, worldly pleasures etc. (cf. *Gen* 3:5-6).

- Souls who already strive for a virtuous life, that is, those who do not look back, but forward, the devil tempts with exaggerated concentration on oneself. This leads either to discouragement, showing the difficulty in progress, the lack of recognition by others, etc. or it leads to proud thoughts, thinking how good one is, comparing and rejecting others as lazy, etc. (cf. *Lk* 18:11-12).

- Souls who seek just the union with the Will of God, like Saint Faustina, the devil does not know how to attack, and so he

---

[100] CONGREGATION OF DIVINE WORSHIP, *Directory on Popular Piety and Liturgy*, 217.

tries in any way possible, without logic, in unreasonable and unexpected ways.[101]

(3) Finally, because "Satan disguises himself as an angel of light" (*2Cor* 11:14), it will always be difficult to discern if man stands under the influence of the fallen spirits. Certain characteristics aid in that discernment.

As a general rule, looking at the fruits according to the indication of Jesus (cf. *Mt* 7:16-20), Saint Augustine wrote:

> Two cities have been formed by two loves: the earthly by the love of self, even to the contempt of God; the heavenly by the love of God, even to the contempt of self. The former, in a word, glories in itself; the latter, in the Lord.[102]

Repeated characteristics of extra-natural or angelic influences can be distinguished that are in part common to both good and fallen Angels. They are:

- *prompt*: the phenomenon appears and disappears suddenly, immediately, instantaneously; comes unexpectedly or 'out of the blue' – not like a natural cause which develops and gradually appears or grows;[103]

---

[101] Cf. J. AUMANN, *Spiritual Theology*, Huntington, IN 1980, 158-162, 243-244; St. JOHN OF THE CROSS, *Spiritual Canticle*, 16, 2.
[102] St. AUGUSTINE, *City of God*, XIV, 28.
[103] Cf. for ex. *Dan* 14:36-39; *Lk* 2:13; *Acts* 12:23.

- *powerful*: also a good Angel may come powerfully, but always with the respect before man;[104]

- *persistently*: the good Angel may show a certain persistence, as he came twice to Elijah (*1Kgs* 19:5-8), but – in contrast to the fallen angels – keeps silence when man rejects his help, and

- *perverse*: this last characteristic makes it easy to discern the influence of a fallen angel from a holy Angel; however, it may not be evident right at the beginning.

To put the concrete characteristics of the angelic manifestations in the light of the general principle, we ask for the realization or the "fruits", that is, if the final end of a proposal will lead to the glory of God or of self.

To benefit from the testimony of Saint Faustina, her experiences can be structured according the following questions:

Whom does the devil attack? where? and when?

How does he attack?

How can man defend himself against the attacks of the fallen angels?

---

[104] See the "Commander of the army of the Lord" (*Josh* 5:13-15) or St. Gabriel to Zechariah (Lk 1:11-20).

6.2 WHOM DOES THE DEVIL ATTACK? WHERE? AND WHEN?

6.2.1. WHOM DOES THE DEVIL ATTACK?

The battle of the devil is concentrated, in a special way, on the *bishops and priests*. Jesus Himself foretold Peter: "Simon, Simon, behold, Satan demanded to have you, that he might sift you like wheat" (*Lk* 22:31). St. Faustina speaks of the

> ... devil's traps and snares which are continually being set for the souls of priests (D. 1052; cf. D. 1384).

Then the enemy pursues especially those persons who want to belong exclusively to God, and those who are in the *state of consecrated life*:

> I saw a great light and a great darkness over house and chapel. I saw the struggle of these two powers (D. 307; cf. D. 1127).

Of course, as Adam and Eve were "tempted by the devil" (CCC 397), so all souls are tempted. The "intelligent and free creatures must journey toward their ultimate destinies by their free choice and preferential love" (CCC 311). The more one tries to live the baptismal and Christian vocation, the more one must depend on them, because

> "the dragon was angry with the woman, and went off to make war on the rest of her offspring, on those who keep the commandments of God and bear testimony to Jesus" (*Rev* 12:17).

However, it is also true that those who have a *special mission* in the kingdom of God, like Saint Faustina, will have to experience still more the special anger of the fallen spirits, as we have already seen.

6.2.2 WHERE DOES THE DEVIL ATTACK?

Did the enemy show special preference where he would attack Saint Faustina? Or are there special places to which he would not have permission to access? Does he have less access to a sacred place like the Church with the Eucharistic Presence of Jesus?

Saint Faustina was attacked by the enemy almost everywhere and unexpectedly.

He appeared when she walked through the convent, "when I was going upstairs" (D. 1405), or when she was in her cell, "Satan rushed into my room with great anger and fury"[105].

Once she was taken by surprise on the street, demons blocked her way (cf. D. 418, 873).

Even on the sacred place, in the chapel, he manifested his presence:

> About midday, I entered the chapel for a moment ... As I continued in a state of recollection, Satan took a flowerpot and angrily hurled it to the ground with all his might. I saw all his rage and his jealousy (D. 411).

---

[105] D. 713; cf. D. 412, 1583.

6.2.3. WHEN DOES THE DEVIL ATTACK?

We can discern certain preferences relating to the time in which the devil tends to approach. Like a thief he prefers the darkness of the night. "Every one who does evil hates the light, and does not come to the light, lest his deeds should be exposed" (Jn 3:20). Nevertheless, the enemy tries, in all possible ways, to separate the souls from God, and so it seems that to him any time is possible.

Going through the notes of Saint Faustina in her *Diary*, one finds that the demons approached her more frequently at night[106] when "it was already eleven o'clock at night, and there was silence all around" (D. 1497).

But her enemies could disturb her in the morning on the way to Mass (cf. D. 873) as well as at noon (cf. D. 411).

In addition, there seems to be no occupation in which the fallen spirits could not appear and cause her troubles. She told about her enemies' attack when she wrote "about the goodness of God" (D. 1338) and His mercy[107].

They could bother her during devotions, "during meditation" (D. 173) or when she was praying for priests (cf. D. 1405). The hours she prayed for the salvation of certain souls were hours of special attacks. She wrote, she "fought a battle with the spirits of darkness over one soul" (D. 812).

---

[106] cf. D. 412, 713, 1405.
[107] cf. D. 1115, 1583, 1659.

This happens especially at the hour of death[108], just as the Council of Trent taught and is mentioned above.[109]

According to Saint Faustina's experience, other times or moments can be identified when the devil attacks with greater facility than in others.

It is when the soul grows "a bit negligent [and does] not pay attention to these interior inspirations" (D. 130). She says: "He has the easiest access ... to lazy and idle souls"[110].

And when the enemy does not succeed through fatigue or inattention, then he tries to attack from outside. When "Satan himself can do no harm, he uses people" (D. 1384), instigates, and "sometimes tempts good people violently, so that they may hinder the work" (D. 1659). We may recall here the wives of Tobit (cf. *Tob* 2:14) and Job (cf. *Job* 2:9) and even St. Peter (cf. *Mt* 16:21-23). Therefore, Sister Faustina needed to be attentive particularly when someone was angry at

---

[108] cf. D. 48, 601, 1479, 1485, 1565, 1798.

[109] Cf. 5.2.2; "Although 'our adversary seeks' and seizes throughout our entire life occasions 'to devour' [*1 Pet* 5:8] our souls in every manner, yet there is no time when he directs earnestly all the strength of his cunning to ruin us completely, and if possible to drive us also from faith in the divine mercy, than when he sees that the end of life is upon us" (DENZINGER, *The Sources of Catholic Dogma*, translated by R. J. Deferrari, Herder, London 1957, 907; DENZINGER-HÜNERMANN, 1694).

[110] D. 1127, cf. D. 1340, CCC 2733.

her, because "Satan always takes advantage of such moments"[111].

Finally, she also observed as dangerous moments, when "God has hidden himself from" (D. 96) her; that is in times of a spiritual desert. In these moments, the enemy can try to win over the soul by troubling it from within, for example, by "... a multitude of thoughts" (D. 644), because "Satan wants just this: to have the person who is aspiring for sanctity direct himself" (D. 938). On the contrary, Jesus told her to "**never trust in yourself**" (D. 1760).

6.3 HOW DOES THE DEVIL ATTACK?

Let us now look at the more important question: "how" does the devil attack souls? What does the experience of this Saint tell us?

6.3.1 SENSIBLE ATTACKS

Clearly, "Satan's anger is terrible ... He is beginning to attack me openly and with such great fury and hate"[112]. Faustina reports one of these cases:

> About midday, I entered the chapel for a moment. ... As I continued in a state of recollection, Satan took a flowerpot and angrily hurled it to the ground with all his might. I saw all his rage and his jealousy.

---

[111] D. 129; cf. W. WILTON, *The Stairway to Perfection*, Image Books, New York, NY 1979, ch. 37-40.
[112] D. 713; cf. D. 412, 419, 520, 540, 1583.

There was no one in the chapel, so I got up, picked up the pieces of the flowerpot, [and] repotted the flower ... (D. 411, 412).

Sometimes we only have the impression that he acts in a particular way:

[In the] evening, ... Satan rushed into my room with great anger and fury. He seized the screen and began to break and crush it ... and yet the screen was not shattered or broken[113].

Among these exterior sensible manifestations of the devils, we have to place others that are impressive and are at the same time like foam; they disappear at one moment if the soul reacts well.[114] Here is an example:

After the adoration, half way to my cell, I was surrounded by a pack of huge black dogs who were jumping and howling and trying to tear me to pieces. I realized that they were not dogs, but demons. ... And they vanished like dust, like the noise of the road (D. 320).

Here appears also a phenomenon found in Sacred Scripture's description of events in paradise, when the serpent, an animal, spoke.[115] Similarly, the devil manifested himself at different times in the form of a cat:

---

[113] D. 713; cf. D. 323, 540.
[114] Cf. St. THOMAS AQ., *Summa Theologiae*, p. I, q. 51, a. 2: "Whether angels assume bodies?".
[115] Cf. *Gen* 3:1ff; cf. later the ass of Balaam, *Num* 22:27-34.

I saw many demons. One of these tried to vex me; taking the form of a cat, he kept throwing himself onto my bed and on my feet, and he was quite heavy, as if [weighing] [sic] a ton (D. 412).

... as I was going to the chapel to attend Holy Mass, I suddenly saw a huge juniper tree on the pavement and in it a horrible cat who, looking angrily at me, blocked my way to the chapel (D. 873).

Then, Saint Faustina speaks of *ugly monsters*:

In the evening when I was writing, I heard a voice in my cell. ... When I looked in the direction of the voice, I saw nothing, and I continued to write. Suddenly I heard a noise and ... I glanced around and saw many ugly monsters ... (D. 540; cf. D. 713).

Saint Thomas Aquinas tries to give a reason for these ugly manifestations of the devil. In his commentary on the book of Job, he makes a reference to the two animals, the greatest one on earth and the greatest one of the sea; this is how he reasons:

Just as through sin man falls from the dignity of reason and acting against reason is compared to irrational creatures, so the devil, too, turning away through sin from the supreme and intelligible goods when he sought primacy over inferior earthly things is compared to brute animals in whose likeness demons frequently appear to men, with God providing that they may be permitted to assume the kinds of shapes of body through which their condition may be designated.[116]

Further, the enemies appeared to Saint Faustina in other forms: "Suddenly, my cell was filled with black figures full of anger and hatred for me" (D. 323).

Once the enemy took on "the form of an apparition" (D. 1465) or phantasm, then in a form of "a soul" which the Saint could unmask only by the pride in its words:

> During the night, a soul I had already seen before visited me. However, it did not ask for prayer, but reproached me, saying that I used to be very haughty and vain[117].

On another occasion, she heard the demon, but afterwards "the voice took the appearance of my Guardian Angel" (D. 1405).

The lives of great Saints such as Saint Benedict, Saint Francis of Assisi, Saint Theresa of Avila or Saint Padre Pio give testimony of these phenomena, confirming what Saint Paul already

---

[116] Cf. St. THOMAS AQ., *The Literal Exposition on Job*, Scholars Press, Atlanta, Georgia 1989, to *Job* 40:15-32, pp. 447-457, 448.

[117] D. 520. This experience explains the prohibition of any form of divination: "There shall not be found among you ... any one who practices divination, a soothsayer, or an augur, or a sorcerer, or a charmer, or a medium, or a wizard, or a necromancer" (*Dt* 18:10-11; cf. CCC 2115-2117).

mentioned, that we should not "wonder, for even Satan disguises himself as an angel of light"[118].

God permits such more noble forms of manifestations so that the devil could deceive us more easily. After discovering the hidden cause, man confesses like Saint Faustina: The soul "sees what it does not want to see. It hears what it does not want to hear. And, oh, it is a terrible thing at times ..." (D. 97). These are strong influences upon the perception of man, but they can be overcome with the grace of the Holy Spirit.

To these phenomena belong also just physical manifestations like sicknesses.

> A sudden illness - a mortal suffering. It was not death ..., but a taste of the suffering of death ... Suddenly, I felt sick, I gasped for breath, there was darkness before my eyes, my limbs grew numb – and there was a terrible suffocation (D. 321).

One characteristic of them is that they appear and disappear suddenly, just like the enemy who causes them. Therefore, she could write the day after this "mortal suffering" (D. 321): "The next day, I felt very weak, but experienced no further suffering" (D. 324).

---

[118] *2Cor* 11:14. Cf. for ex. for St. Padre Pio da Pietrelcina: A. PARENTE, "*Send me Your Guardian Angel*" Padre Pio, Parto, PA, 1984, 38-41 and Marco TOSATTI, *Padre Pio e il Diavolo. Gabriele Amorth Racconta* ..., Edizioni Piemme, Casale Monferrato, 2003.

6.3.2 TOUCHING THE EMOTIONS

Saint Faustina also suffered from demonic attacks directed against her emotional state:

> Satan always takes advantage of such moments; thoughts of discouragement began to rise to the surface ... I broke out in a sweat, and fear began to overcome me. I had no one to lean on interiorly (D. 129).

On another occasion:

> ... since early in the morning, my soul has been in darkness. ... an extraordinary disgust with life came over me (D. 1496, 1497).

> ... a strange dislike for everything having to do with God (D. 1405).

> I felt a strange fear that the priest would not understand me, or that he would have no time to hear everything (D. 173).

The fallen angels recognize human nature as the substantial union of spiritual soul and physical body, as a psychosomatic reality. This knowledge brings mutual influence with it. As ideas provoke both emotional and physical reactions, emotions influence not only one's thinking but also one's will and actions. Saint Faustina tells us that in a moment of spiritual darkness, the devil can awaken ideas contrary to God, to His love and to His will. Then, hearing interior words like: "You have been rejected by God!" (D. 98) she perceives something like:

> ... fire which penetrates every nerve to the marrow of the bone. It pierces right through

> her entire being. ... The soul ... shrinks into itself and loses sight of everything; it is as though it has accepted the torture of being abandoned. This is a moment for which I have no words. This is the agony of the soul (D. 98).

These emotional clouds serve only to weaken the soul and her will; they are followed by spiritual attacks. It seems that a war had been started in her soul, a war of thoughts and feelings.

> Various defects and imperfections rise up within it, and it must fight them furiously. All her faults lift up their heads, but the soul's vigilance is great. The former awareness of the presence of God gives place to coldness and spiritual dryness; the soul has no taste for spiritual exercises; it cannot pray, either in the old way, or in the manner in which it had just begun to pray. It struggles this way and that, but can find no satisfaction. God has hidden Himself from it, and it can find no consolation in creatures, nor can any of these creatures find a way of consoling it. The soul craves passionately for God, but sees its own misery; it begins to sense God's justice; it seems to it that it has lost all the gifts that God had given it; its mind is dimmed, and darkness fills it; unspeakable torment begins. The soul tries to explain its state to the confes- sor, but it is not understood and is assailed by an even greater unrest. [Then] Satan begins his work (D. 96).

An expiatory offering like Saint Faustina's "act of oblation" opens the soul for such influences of the enemies; they are then part of the spiritual battle.

> When I received permission from my confessor [Father Sopocko] to make an act of oblation, I soon learned that it was pleasing to God, because I immediately began to experience its effects. In a moment my soul became like a stone – dried up, filled with torment, and disquiet. ... Distrust and despair invaded my heart. This is the condition of the poor people, which I have taken upon myself (D. 311).

The effect of these interior changes can lead the soul to mental exhaustion and fatigue. Doubt can also easily grow under these conditions (cf. D. 1086). In fact, this doubt is used by the devil like a "worm" on his fishing-rod, as it is since paradise[119].

> I began to grow a bit negligent. I did not pay attention to these interior inspirations and tried to distract myself (D. 130).

The Saint "could see what was going on" in her soul; she realized that it is a spiritual battle and that she needed to bring it into the light of reason and speak up to someone in order to avert the net which the enemy was about to weave around her soul. She opened up in confession.

> But ... I resolved to put an end to these doubts of mine before my perpetual vows. ... I prayed

---

[119] Cf. *Gen* 3:1-6; and for the New Testament cf. *Lk* 1:18 and the beginning of the Church cf. *Jn* 20:25; *Mt* 28:17. St. James says "he who doubts is like a wave of the sea that is driven and tossed by the wind" (*Jas* 1:6).

for light for the priest to whom I was to open up my soul to its depths (D. 131).

When the soul's strength of will is weakened, and it is inattentive, then there is a great danger that it will consent to temptations. One example would be to believe that we have made bad choices in our life, and that we should change our state of life and leave our marriage or the religious life.

6.3.3 "A MULTITUDE OF THOUGHTS"

In this climate, the enemy also bombs the soul with a "multitude of thoughts" (D. 644), a swarm of confusing ideas, ridicule, and accusing sins, threatening with suffering and confusion, deviating from the will of God, from prayer, from the confessor, sometimes with very subtle arguments.

> Satan tried to persuade me into believing that if my superiors have told me that my inner life is an illusion, why should I ask again and trouble the confessor? Didn't M.X. ... tell you that the Lord Jesus does not commune with souls as miserable as yours? ... and Mother X told you that all this communing with the Lord Jesus was day dreaming and pure hysteria. ... You would do better to dismiss all this as illusions (D. 173).

There is no occasion which would not serve him for his attacks. Once, after a confession in which the priest put her to the test: "Sister, this is an illusion. ... Everything" (D. 643), the following happened.

> When I left the confessional, a multitude of thoughts oppressed my soul. ... I entered into a

kind of agony. I did not feel the presence of God, but all the justice of God weighed heavily upon me. I saw myself as if knocked down for the sins of the world. Satan began to mock me. "See, now you will no longer strive to win souls; look how you've been paid! Nobody will believe you that Jesus demands this. See ... how much more you are going to suffer! After all, the confessor has now released you from all these things" (D. 644).

Even though the list is long, it may be worthwhile to mention what the Saint heard from the enemy, who attempted to destroy her peace and thus influence her decisions: personal offenses, false accusations, immoral proposals, attempts to deviate from her vocation and mission, insinuations against the confessors, confused and malicious reasoning, attacks against God Himself, the truths of Christian faith, especially with regard to Divine Mercy and the salvation of souls.

Here are some examples:

- Satan says to it, "Look, no one understands you; why speak about all this?" Words that terrify it sound in its ears, and it seems to the soul that it is uttering these against God (D. 97).

- All sorts of blasphemies and curses kept pressing upon my ears. ... During the first ... confession, I was set at peace (D. 311; cf. D. 673).

- Look how many humiliations you have suffered because of them, and how many more are still awaiting you, and all the sisters know that you are a hysteric (D. 173).

- You see, to live as a good nun, it is sufficient to live like all the others. Why expose yourself to so many difficulties? (D. 1497).

- I see that you are suffering very much at this moment. I'm going to give you a piece of advice on which your happiness will depend: Never speak about God's mercy ... because they deserve a just punishment (D. 1497; cf. D. 1580).

- ... reproached me, saying that I used to be very haughty and vain[120] ... "and now you are interceding for others while you yourself still have certain vices" (D. 520).

- See how contradictory everything is that Jesus gives to you: He tells you to found a convent, and then He gives you sickness; He tells you to set about establishing this Feast of Mercy while the whole world does not ... want such a feast. Why do you pray for this feast? It is so inopportune (D. 1497).

- Think no more about this work. God is not as merciful as you say He is (D. 1405).

- Do not pray for sinners, because they will be damned all the same, and by this work of mercy you expose your own self to damnation (D. 1405).

---

[120] This is a typical form of temptation: recalling, and accusing of past sins.

- Talk no more about this mercy of God with your confessor and especially not with Father Sopocko and Father Andrasz (D. 1405).

- The priest would not understand me ... Didn't [Mother] M.X. tell you ... This confessor is going to tell you the same thing. Why speak to him about all this? These are not sins, ... why tell it to this confessor? (D. 173).

- Another very important thing: do not tell your confessors, and especially this extraordinary confessor and the priest in Vilnius, about what goes on in your soul. I know them; I know who they are, and so I want to put you on your guard against them[121].

- Why be sincere? (D. 644).

- ... thoughts of discouragement began to rise to the surface - for your faithfulness and sincerity - this is your reward. How can one be sincere when one is so misunderstood? (D. 129).

- Why should you bother about other souls? You ought to be praying only for yourself. As for sinners, they will be converted without your prayers (D. 1497; cf. D. 1768).

- Do not pray for sinners, but for yourself, for you will be damned (D. 1465).

- Ask for death for yourself, tomorrow after Holy Communion. God will hear you, for He has

---

[121] D. 1497; that is: sowing doubts, mistrust, division.

heard you so many times before and has given you that which you asked of Him (D. 1497).

- "You see, God is so Holy, and you are sinful. Do not approach Him, and go to Confession every day." And indeed, whatever I thought of seemed to me to be a sin. ... I understood that Satan, wanting to disturb my peace, has been giving me exaggerated thoughts (D. 1802; cf. D. 429).

- Faith staggers under the impact; the struggle is fierce. The soul tries hard to cling to God by an act of will. With God's permission, Satan goes even further: hope and love are put to the test. These temptations are terrible. God supports the soul in secret, so to speak. The soul is not aware of this, but otherwise it would be impossible to stand firm; and God knows very well how much He can allow to befall a soul. The soul is tempted to unbelief in respect to revealed truths and to insincerity towards the confessor (D. 97; cf. D. 1558).

- But this is not yet the end of the testing; there is still the trial of trials, the complete abandonment of the soul by God (D. 97).

- The ordeal reaches its climax. The soul no longer looks for help anywhere. It shrinks into itself and loses sight of everything; it is as though it has accepted the torture of being abandoned (D. 98).

At the end and in conclusion, the tempter wants to eternally separate the soul from God. He wants to occupy His place in the souls and in life. "All these I will give you, if you will fall down and worship me" (Mt 4:9). Something similar occurred to Saint Faustina in 1935.

> A soul continued to reproach me, saying, "Why are you unwilling to recognize my greatness? Why do you alone not glorify me for my great deeds as all others do?" Then I saw that this was Satan under the assumed appearance of this soul (D. 520).

Saint Faustina persevered through this difficult experience. She was attentive to the different movements of the tempter, which, so far, had all been "just" temptations, although they were very persistent in knocking at the soul's door.

Thomas à Kempis described this sequence: "First, a mere thought comes to mind, then strong imagination, followed by pleasure, evil delight, and consent"[122] which would constitute a sin. However, Faustina did not permit him to pass "the door of her soul."

God "will sit as a refiner and purifier of silver, and he will purify the sons of Levi and refine them like gold and silver, until they present right offerings to the Lord" (Mal 3:3). Saint Faustina clearly referenced this quote when she wrote about the meaning of this in the plan of God:

---

[122] THOMAS A KEMPIS, *Imitation of Christ*, I, 13. Here we should remember C. S. Lewis' masterpiece that presents in theory what St. Faustina told from personal experience: *The Screwtape Letters. How a Senior Devil Instructs a Junior Devil in the Art of Temptation*, Macmillan Publishing Co., New York, NY 1961.

All these trials are heavy and difficult. God does not send them to a soul which has not already been admitted to a deeper intimacy with Him and which has not yet tasted the divine delights. Besides, in this God has His own plans, which for us are impenetrable. God often prepares a soul in this way for His future designs and great works. He wants to try it as pure gold is tried (D. 97).

The Faith guarantees us that God never loses control of the history of mankind, nor of the life of any individual person (cf. Mt 10:30-31). This, however, does not prevent Him from testing man or permitting the temptation to evil. Do not we humans act exactly the same way in all areas of life? Do we not test any object or machine before we use it or any food or drink before we take it? Moreover, the more important it is, the stronger, the test and the more precise the measure. This is the meaning of these temptations.

6.4 HOW CAN MAN DEFEND HIMSELF AGAINST THE ATTACKS OF THE FALLEN ANGELS?

Now it is important to ask Saint Faustina how to defend oneself against the attacks of the fallen spirits. What was her attitude? Despair? Discouragement? Not at all. God "knows what the soul can endure" (D. 101), she affirmed, and therefore walked before Him with confidence and hope, as well as with patience, fortitude and perseverance;

always impelled by love of God, the Saint looked forward.

> I know well that the wretch will not touch me without God's willing it, but what is he up to? He is beginning to attack me openly and with such great fury and hate, but he does not disturb my peace for a moment, and this composure of mine makes him furious (D. 713);
>
> I sensed the hostility of the enemy of souls, but he did not touch me (D. 1646).

And what a declaration of war we can see in this confession.

> Oh, how sweet it is to toil for God and souls! I want no respite in this battle, but I shall fight to the last breath for the glory of my King and Lord. I shall not lay the sword aside until He calls me before His throne; I fear no blows, because God is my shield. It is the enemy who should fear us, and not we him. Satan defeats only the proud and the cowardly, because the humble are strong. Nothing will confuse or frighten a humble soul. I have directed my flight at the very center of the sun's heat, and nothing can lower its course. Love will not allow itself to be taken prisoner; it is free like a queen. Love attains God (D. 450).

6.4.1 HE SEEKS "LAZY AND IDLE SOULS"

St. Paul alerts the Ephesians to take care that they do not confront the devil: "Give no opportunity to the devil" (*Eph* 4:27). Saint Faustina related one encounter with the devil where he revealed to her that he seeks lazy souls, referring to "sloth or acedia", one of the seven Capital sins.[123]

> On one occasion, I saw Satan hurrying about and looking for someone among the sisters, but he could find no one. I felt an interior inspiration to command him in the Name of God to confess to me what he was looking for among the sisters. And he confessed, though unwillingly, "I am looking for idle souls [cf. *Si.* 33:28; *Pr.* 12:11]." When I commanded him again in the Name of God to tell me to which souls in the religious life he has the easiest access, he said, again unwillingly, "To lazy and idle souls." I took note of the fact that, at present, there were no such souls in this house. Let the toiling and tired souls rejoice (D. 1127).

However, one can not and should not trust oneself:

I want to teach you about spiritual warfare. Never trust in yourself, but abandon yourself totally to My will (D. 1760).

At some point, man is submitted in this life to the test, and he "can therefore go astray" (CCC 311). Prudence demands that we arm ourselves with weapons for defense in the spiritual battle. Saint Faustina helps us in identifying a temptation. From her life we will also find different ways to defeat the devil.

---

[123] Cf. CCC 1866; 2733; St. Thomas Aq., *Summa Theologiae*, p. II-II, q. 35.

6.4.2 SILENCE

The first reaction, which is very decisive at the beginning of an attack, is to use silence to ignore the temptation, or to refuse to listen to the devil's arguments. Do not become involved with the evil, but let God's light reveal the truth.

The Saint conversed only three times with the devil, but not without verifying God's permission: at the occasion in the convent we just saw (cf. D. 1127), at her return from the Holy Hour (cf. D. 320), and on the following occasion:

> ... a great multitude of demons blocked my way ... and voices could be heard: "She has snatched away everything we have worked for over so many years!" When I asked them, "Where have you come from in such great numbers?" the wicked forms answered, "Out of human hearts; stop tormenting us!" (D. 418).

It is true, that the devils were about to lose and implored Saint Faustina, "stop tormenting us!" But on the other occasion, we can see the caution she showed in exchanging phrases, because she knew that "he is a liar and the father of lies" (Jn 8:44). Jesus acted with firmness in this point: "Be silent!" (Mk 1:25); "and He would not permit the demons to speak" (Mk 1:34; cf. 3:12). On the contrary, Eve in paradise allowed a conversation with the devil, which caused the terrible catastrophe for all her descendants (cf. Gen 3:1-7).

In general, the reaction of Saint Faustina, exactly in the midst of the "words of the tempter", was silence; she gave him the cold shoulder and turned to God, and this in spite of having experienced that the devil had to obey her (cf. D. 741). Her equilibrium and prudence are especially eloquent in our day, so much marked by confusion in this area.

> My soul remained silent and, by an act of will, continued to pray without entering into conversation with the Spirit of Darkness ... I remained silent and, by an act of will, I began to pray, or rather, submitted myself to God, asking Him interiorly not to abandon me at this moment (D. 1497).

It was still a frightful silence, imploring the help of God. Afterwards, she became more and more courageous:

> I remained silent, and by an act of will I dwelt in God, although a moan escaped from my heart. Finally, the tempter went away (D. 1498).

It is not a silence of fear, or of flight; it is also not a strategy to ignore the enemy or a question of a game. Rather, it is a decision and conscious rejection, in a certain sense a disregard and contempt for him. Jesus gave her this instruction: **"Do not bargain with any temptation"**[124].

---

[124] D. 1760. Saint Padre Pio related once to his Spiritual Director, Padre Agostino: "When I received your letter recently and before I had opened it, those *wretches* told me to tear it up or else throw it in the fire. If I did this, they would withdraw for good and would never trouble me again. I kept

Isn't this similar to daily life? When the doorbell rings and we see a thief standing there, the door remains closed and no explanation is necessary.

It was Jesus himself who confirmed to her the importance of this attitude, the value of silence:

> Jesus ... said, **I am pleased with what you are doing. ... Satan gained nothing by tempting you, because you did not enter into conversation with him. Continue to act in this way. You gave Me great glory today by fighting so faithfully** (D. 1499).

Positively, this silence, in relation to the devil, opens the space and underlines the necessity for an always more intense search for God and distance from evil. It is God Who merits to be listened to, not the evil one. This must be the "fruit" of all tests and why one theologian put it, therefore, in very smart words: After God, no one contributes more to our sanctification, the search

---

silent without giving them any answer, while in my heart I despised them. Then they added: 'We want this merely as a condition for our withdrawal. In doing so you will not be showing contempt for anyone.' I replied that nothing would make me change my mind. They flung themselves upon me like so many hungry tigers, cursing me and threatening to make me pay for it." (St. PADRE PIO OF PIETRELCINA, *Letters*, vol. I, San Giovanni Rotondo, ²1984, 376 f). Someone's bumper sticker says: "When Satan knocks on your door, have Jesus answer it for you" (Deborah LIPSKY, *A Message of Hope. Confessions of an Ex-Satanist: How to Protect Yourself from Evil*, Tau, Phoenix, AZ 2012, 178).

for God, than the one who wants it least, that is the devil.[125]

Therefore, once we learn to keep distance from the enemy, the practice of walking in the presence of God is the next most powerful means of our defense. "If it is by the finger of God that I cast out demons, then the kingdom of God has come upon you" (*Lk* 11:20). As ministers of God, His faithful Angels are sent into the spiritual battle and overcome all diabolic attacks if God wishes it.

God Himself is the secret of all other weapons, namely, of the profession of faith, the sacraments, prayer and use of sacramentals as well as the obedience towards the representatives of God, especially a Spiritual Director.

6.4.3 *"THE ALMIGHTY IS WITH HER!"*

Saint Faustina discovered that the devil flees from the presence of God. She understood when she suffered "the complete abandonment of the soul by God"[126]: There was nothing left of her; God alone remained.

This was the greatest lesson she learned: How much she is nothing, and that only God is all.

It was after that Thursday's Holy Hour in which she "called upon the whole of heaven to

---

[125] "No one, after God, has contributed so much to the sanctification of Job than the devil, and no one wanted this less" (Charles JOURNET, *Le mal, essai théologique*, Paris 1962, 282; quoted in G. HUBER, *Vattene via, Satana! Il diavolo oggi*, Libreria Editrice Vaticana, Roma 1992, 61).

[126] D. 97; cf. D. 98, 496.

join me in making amends to the Lord for the ingratitude of certain souls" (D. 319). After that, "half way to my cell, I was surrounded by a pack of huge black dogs" (D. 320) she realized were demons.

> One of them spoke up in a rage, "Because you have snatched so many souls away from us this night, we will tear you to pieces" (ibid.).

The Saint responded, just coming from prayer:

> I answered, "If that is the will of the most merciful God, tear me to pieces, for I have justly deserved it, because I am the most miserable of all sinners, and God is ever holy, just and infinitely merciful" (ibid.).

Her humility and, even more, the reference to God and His will, not so much as a refuge, but more as confession of faith, smashed these very wild enemies:

> To these words all the demons answered as one, "Let us flee, for she is not alone; the Almighty is with her!" And they vanished like dust, like the noise of the road, while I continued on my way to my cell undisturbed, finishing my *Te Deum* and pondering the infinite and unfathomable mercy of God[127].

This is the pure truth that the Saint observed in such a tangible way: Anyone who surrenders himself to the Will of God and lives in conformity with it falls into the hands of the Almighty. And

---

[127] D. 320; cf. D. 1488, 1570.

He will enkindle the divine light in the soul, like St. Michael did when he said in the darkness of the test of the Angels: "*Who is like God!*" This light and its strength expelled and will always expel anything that tries to oppose God. This is the counsel of St. James: "Submit yourselves therefore to God. Resist the devil and he will flee from you"[128].

> These dreadful thoughts tormented me throughout the whole hour. ... I submitted to the will of God and repeated, "O God, let whatever You have decided upon happen to me. Nothing in me is any longer my own." Then, suddenly, God's presence enveloped me and penetrated me through and through[129].

> And when I see his great fury, I stay inside the stronghold; that is, the Most Sacred Heart of Jesus (D. 1287; cf. D. 1535).

> I heard a voice within my soul, "**Do not fear; I am with you**". And an unusual light illumined my mind, and I understood that I should not give in to such sorrows (D. 129).

> **He who trusts in My mercy will not perish, for all his affairs are Mine, and his enemies**

---

[128] *James* 4:7; cf. what David said to Abishai and to all his servants before Shimei: "Let him curse; for the Lord has bidden him. It may be that the Lord will look upon my affliction, and that the Lord will repay me with good for this cursing of me today" (*2Sam* 16:11-12).

[129] D. 644; cf. D. 666, 674, 1411, 1720.

will be shattered at the base of My footstool (D. 723; cf. D. 480).

Through the sacrament of *Baptism* something new happens to our human nature: "The baptized person belongs no longer to himself, but to Him who died and rose for us" (CCC 1269). In this way, the baptized is called to follow the example of all those who knew to say "Yes" to the Divine Word and Presence, day by day. Among them stand out Our Lady, Mary, the Mother of Jesus who "responds by offering her whole being: 'Behold I am the handmaid of the Lord; let it be [done] to me according to your word'." (CCC 2617). Only in this way, the Christian becomes able to say this most perfect "Christian prayer: to be wholly God's, because he is wholly ours" (ibid.). It is the most effective shield against evil. What a great power we have at our disposal: to always accept and confirm this "Fiat!" of the Blessed Virgin Mary.

> The soul tries hard to cling to God by an act of will.[130]

6.4.4 THE HOLY ANGELS

God gave men help through Our Lady. He said to Saint Faustina: "**ask My Mother and the Saints for help**" (D. 1560; cf. D. 79). And our Saint believed and prayed:

> O Mary, Immaculate Virgin,
> Pure crystal for my heart,
> You are my strength, O sturdy anchor!

---

[130] D. 97; cf. D. 1496, 1497.

> You are a shield and protection for a weak heart (D. 161).

God was also present in the life of Saint Faustina through His powerful holy Angels. Because of the great hatred of the demons against the Saint, God asked Saint Michael "to take special care" (D. 706) of her. The Archangel communicated this to sister. In the same "visit" he confirmed the hatred of the evil, but assured her too that she should "not fear" (ibid.).

At the gate of the Convent God, "**set a Cherub over it to guard it**" (D. 1271). And with this, she heard the invitation: "**Be at peace!**" (ibid.).

Once, Saint Faustina writes: "I feel that there is a power which is defending me and protecting me from the blows of the enemy" (D. 1799). Here it is difficult to determine what "power" she refers to; however, it seems to be a person acting, and so very probably it might be a specific Angel.

More frequently, Saint Faustina could speak about the help she received concretely from her *Guardian Angel*. Once, she called for his help against the demons and immediately experienced the powerful defense against the devils through her Guardian Angel. His immediate manifestation made the disturbance cease and also, the fallen angels to immediately disappear. Further, the Guardian Angel added these encouraging words which have permanent value:

> "Do not fear, spouse of my Lord; without [God's] permission these spirits will do you no harm" (D. 419).

On another occasion, she prayed to her Angel, and he seemed to get control over everything, so that she could be at peace:

> I fell asleep as soon as I lay down, but at about eleven o'clock Satan shook my bed. I awoke instantly, and I started to pray peacefully to my Guardian Angel. Then I saw the souls who were doing penance in purgatory. They appeared like shadows, and among them I saw many demons. One of these tried to vex me; taking the form of a cat, he kept throwing himself onto my bed and on my feet, and he was quite heavy, as if (weighing) [sic] a ton.
>
> I kept praying the rosary all the while, and toward dawn these beings vanished, and I was able to get some sleep. When I entered the chapel in the morning I heard a voice in my soul, "**You are united to Me; fear nothing**" (D. 412).

She also affirms the Angel's help with another person.

> The Lord said to me, **My daughter, help Me to save a certain dying sinner. Say the chaplet that I have taught you for him.** When I began to say the chaplet, I saw the man dying in the midst of terrible torment and struggle. His Guardian Angel was defending him ... (D. 1565).

This was God's intention when He told Moses:

> Behold, I send an Angel before you, to guard you on the way and to bring you to the place

which I have prepared. ... If you hearken attentively to his voice and do all that I say, then I will be an enemy to your enemies and an adversary to your adversaries (*Ex* 23:20,22).

The Church has always encouraged the faithful, both individually and corporately in the official Liturgy, to seek the heavenly fighter, St. Michael, for example, with this prayer:

Send Michael, the prince of the heavenly host, to the aid of your people, may he defend them against Satan and his angels on the day of battle.[131]

The following prayer "was introduced at the end of the [19th] century"[132] by Pope Leo XIII,

---

[131] *Liturgy of the Hours*, Intercessions at the Morning Prayer on October 2nd; cf. *Ritual of Exorcism*, App. II, n. 10.

[132] In his speech for the *Regina caeli* on April 24, 1994, Pope John Paul II said at the end: "May prayer strengthen us for the spiritual battle we are told about in the Letter to the Ephesians 'Draw strength from the Lord and from His mighty power' (*Eph* 6:10). The Book of Revelation refers to this same battle, recalling before our eyes the image of St. Michael the Archangel (*Rev* 12:7). Pope Leo XIII certainly had a very vivid recollection of this scene when he introduced at the end of the last century a special prayer to St. Michael throughout the Church. 'St. Michael the Archangel, defend us in battle, be our safeguard against the wickedness and snares of the devil.' Although today this prayer is no longer recited at the end of Mass, I ask everyone not to forget it, and to recite it to obtain help in the battle against the forces of darkness and against the spirit of this world" (In: *L'Osservatore Romano*, weekly engl. edition, April 27, 1994, page 3).

spread and recently again recommended by Pope John Paul II goes like this:

> St. Michael the Archangel, defend us in battle; be our protection against the wickedness and snares of the devil. May God rebuke him, we humbly pray, and you, O prince of the heavenly host, by the power of God thrust into hell Satan and all the evil spirits who roam about the world, seeking the ruin of souls. Amen.[133]

6.4.5 PROFESSION OF FAITH

Another weapon for the spiritual battle is the simple invocation or mere reference to the name of God. This is verified by the experience of Saint Faustina, particularly when she praised and glorified God. Thus Jesus explains to the Saint:

> **When a soul extols My goodness, Satan trembles before it and flees to the very bottom of hell** (D. 378).

The experience of Saint Faustina confirms this word of the Lord repeatedly. She writes:

> I suddenly saw a huge juniper tree on the pavement and in it a horrible cat ... One whisper of the name of Jesus dissipated all that (D. 873).

> I said, "Glory is due to God alone; begone Satan!" And in an instant this soul fell into an abyss, horrible beyond all description! And I

---

[133] Ibid.

said to the wretched soul that I would tell the whole Church about this (D. 520).

As soon as I said, "And the Word was made flesh and dwelt among us," the figures vanished in a sudden whir (D. 323).

In the Litany to the Divine Mercy we confess and invoke at the same time:

Divine Mercy, shielding us from the fire of hell, I trust in You! (D. 949).

In the light of this experience the purifying, protecting and renewing effect of the old salutation among the faithful is seen: "Praised be Our Lord Jesus Christ!" to which the other responds: "Now and for ever!" With such a custom, we "continually offer up a sacrifice of praise to God" (*Heb* 13:15; cf. *Ps* 106:22) and approach the goal of our vocation, namely to be part of the people who "in Christ have been destined and appointed to live for the praise of his glory" (*Eph* 1:12).

6.4.6 PRAYER, SACRAMENTS, AND SACRAMENTALS

Firm faith makes prayer authentic and effective. In prayer, the soul directs herself to God. She acts with the baptismal grace, so that the power of God strengthens her, or, as Saint Faustina once confessed:

The devils were full of hatred for me, but they had to obey me at the command of God (D. 741).

The soul recognizes, in the spiritual battles, her own nothingness and God as the Creator and Savior (cf. CCC 2096, 2097).

6.4.6.1 PRAYERS

An effect like an exorcism can be observed by the recitation of the *Creed*, the *Our Father*, the *Magnificat* of Our Lady, her *Rosary*[134] and the prayer of the *Angelus* with the powerful reference to the Incarnation of the Son of God, and by other prayers of Christian piety of the past and the presence.[135]

We especially recall the recitation of the official prayer of the Church, or the *Liturgy of the Hours*, "the Divine Office", which is "truly the voice of the Bride herself addressed to her Bridegroom. It is the very prayer which Christ himself with his Body addresses to the Father" (CCC 1174), and which "is intended to become the prayer of the whole People of God" (CCC 1175).

---

[134] Of the Rosary said St. Louis de Montfort: "When people say the Rosary together it is far more formidable to the devil than one said privately, because in this public prayer it is an army that is attacking him" (St. LOUIS DE MONTFORT, *The Secret of the Rosary*, Montfort Publications, Bay Shore, NY 1954, "Forty-Sixth Rose", 98; cf. also ibid., "Thirty-Sixth Rose", 81).

[135] Mention can be still made of the *Stations of the Cross*, the Litany of the Name of Jesus, of the Precious Blood and of All Saints. The *Ritual of Exorcism* mentions some "invocations of the Blessed Virgin Mary," for ex. "Mary, Mother of Grace, Mother of Mercy, protect us from the enemy and receive us in the hour of death" (*Rite of Exorcism*, Appendix II, 9; cf. J. PORTEOUS, *Manual of Minor Exorcisms*, Catholic Truth Society, London 2012).

6.4.6.2 SIGN OF THE CROSS

The *sign of the Cross* also must be mentioned. According to an old tradition, this simple sign is a profession of our faith; it is also a prayer that is able to make all the truths of the faith present, the mystery of God, the Blessed Trinity, our Redemption on the Cross and Holy Baptism. So, Saint Faustina recalls:

> I glanced around and saw many ugly monsters. So I mentally made the Sign of the Cross and they disappeared immediately. How terribly ugly Satan is! (D. 540).

> Satan rushed into my room with great anger and fury. ... I was a little frightened at first, but I immediately made the sign of the cross with my little crucifix, and the beast fell quiet and disappeared at once (D. 713).

> ... at that moment I replied, "I know who you are: the father of lies [cf. Jn. 8:44]." I made the sign of the cross, and the angel vanished with great racket and fury (D. 1405).

The power of this weapon is confirmed in the life of many Saints. Saint Stanislaus Kostka, for example, was "visited" during his sickness by a great black *dog* with flaming eyes, running at his bed. Calmly, the sick saint, using his hand, made the sign of the cross above the monster, and it fell backwards. When the dog approached a second time and a third time, it always whined at the sign, and then it disappeared as suddenly as it appeared.[136]

We need to rediscover urgently some of the lost treasures of Christian Tradition, teaching children from childhood little gestures, which are fruits of the faith, nourishing and protecting it. For example, recall the old custom, blessing oneself with a small sign of the cross first on the forehead, then over the lips and heart and, only then, making a large one, which is the custom today. This sign is accompanied by a prayer which is a small exorcism which should be prayed every day by everyone.

> "Through the sign + of the holy Cross
> free me + from my enemies
> Almighty + God:
> the Father and + the Son and the Holy Spirit!"[137]

Remember, when the devil reacts to a "mental" sign, it is not necessary for us to make the sign over us in critical moments, since by doing this we could unnecessarily call attention to ourselves; it is enough to make it, for example, with our eyes, because the fallen spirits will observe this.

---

[136] F. HOLBÖCK, *Vereint mit den Engeln und Heiligen*, Christiana-Verlag, Stein am Rhein 1984, 334.
[137] Cf. *Rite of Exorcism*, Appendix II. 8.

6.4.6.3 DIVINE MERCY CHAPLET

Among very effective prayers is the *Divine Mercy Chaplet*, which Saint Faustina received from God. Through this prayer, the Angel of the wrath of God became helpless (cf. D. 474-475), and similarly, another Angel was hindered who would have caused "much havoc ... through this storm" (D. 1791) so that Saint Faustina once more "recognized that this prayer was pleasing to God, and that this chaplet was most powerful" (ibid.).

On another occasion she described the victory over the enemies through Christ and this prayer:

> When I entered the chapel for a moment, the Lord said to me, **My daughter, help Me to save a certain dying sinner. Say the chaplet that I have taught you for him.** When I began to say the chaplet, I saw the dying man in the midst of terrible torment and struggle. His Guardian Angel was defending him, but he was, as it were, powerless against the enormity of the soul's misery. A multitude of devils was waiting for the soul. But while I was saying the chaplet, I saw Jesus just as He is depicted in the image. The rays which issued from Jesus' Heart enveloped the sick man, and the powers of darkness fled in panic. The sick man peacefully breathed his last (D. 1565).

6.4.6.4 SACRAMENTS

The enemy of salvation acts with greater facility where sin reigns, especially great sins. The refusal to sin, sincere repentance, and sacramental confession are like a slap in the face to him.[138] The *sacrament of reconciliation* includes an act of humility on the part of the penitent that destroys the pride and influence of the enemy. Saint Faustina says:

> All sorts of blasphemies and curses kept pressing upon my ears. Distrust and despair invaded my heart. ... At first, I was very much frightened by these horrible things, but during the first [opportune] confession, I was set at peace (D. 311; D. 1736).

In Confession, what the enemy has done is brought to light. He abhors light, and therefore flees[139].

> Today after Holy Communion, Jesus again gave me a few directives: **First, do not fight against temptation by yourself, but disclose it to the confessor at once, and then the temptation will lose all its force** (D. 1560).

Saint Faustina constantly gave testimony about the Real Presence of Jesus in the *Holy Eucharist*. The excellence of the most holy Eucharist has been mentioned previously (cf. above 4.2). About its role in the spiritual battle she says:

> Holy Communion assures me that I will win the victory; and so it is (D. 91).

---

[138] Cf. CCC 1447; 1450; 1852-1869; see below to obedience, 6.4.7.
[139] Cf. Jn 3:19-21. St. IGNATIUS OF LOYOLA, *Spiritual Exercises*, n. 326, 13st Rule of Discernment of Spirits.

O Blessed Host, our only hope in the midst of the ravages of the enemy and the efforts of hell (D. 356).

O Blessed Host, take up Your dwelling within my soul, O Thou my heart's purest love! With Your brilliance the darkness dispel (D. 159).

Jesus Himself strengthened her for the spiritual battle.

I find myself so weak that were it not for Holy Communion I would fall continually. One thing alone sustains me, and that is Holy Communion. From it I draw my strength; in it is all my comfort. I fear life on days when I do not receive Holy Communion. I fear my own self. Jesus concealed in the Host is everything to me. From the tabernacle I draw strength, power, courage and light. Here, I seek consolation in time of anguish. I would not know how to give glory to God if I did not have the Eucharist in my heart (D. 1037; cf. D. 1824).

6.4.6.5 HOLY WATER

Holy Water is a sacramental "which recalls Baptism" (CCC 1668). If used with faith, it helps the recipient to receive two principle fruits of baptism. It purifies us from venial sins and some contamination with evil. It renews our union with God through grace; Saint Faustina wrote "holy water is indeed of great help to the dying" (D. 601). The Saint made use of it very spontaneously, even in the presence of a priest, because she saw the demons present:

Once, when one of our sisters became fatally ill and all the community was gathered together, there was also a priest there who gave the sister absolution. Suddenly, I saw many spirits of darkness. Then, forgetting that I was with the sisters, I seized the holy water sprinkler and sprinkled the spirits, and they disappeared at once (D. 601).

6.4.6.6 SUFFERINGS AND PRAYERS

Finally, Saint Faustina still recognized the power of penitential works that accompany prayer, especially suffering:

I saw that my suffering and prayer shackled Satan and snatched many souls from his clutches (D. 1465).

This is a reminder of Jesus' answer to the apostles: Certain kinds of demons never come out "except by prayer and fasting" (Mt 17:21).

6.4.7 OBEDIENCE

St. Paul teaches that Satan can appear like an angel of light. With this statement, he generally refers to all the ways where the evil one hides behind something good. The demon also tried to seduce Saint Faustina in pious forms, as, for example, encouraging her to confess daily or to pray for herself (and not for others). In this hard school of spiritual life, however, she was alerted about such maneuvers when she received still clearer insight:

I felt that the confessor's words were Jesus' words, and although it made me sad to miss Holy Mass, during which God had been granting me the grace of seeing the infant Jesus; nevertheless, I placed obedience above everything else.

I become absorbed in prayer and said my penance. Then I suddenly saw the Lord, who said to me, **My daughter, know that you give Me greater glory by a single act of obedience than by long prayers and mortifications.** Oh, how good it is to live under obedience, to live conscious of the fact that everything I do is pleasing to God! (D. 894)

This is the fundamental lesson:

Satan can even clothe himself in a cloak of humility, but he does not know how to wear the cloak of obedience (D. 939).

Saint Faustina told us how she could save herself – and it was more than once – only through obedience. Speaking of the agony of the soul, she said:

It was only out of obedience to my confessor that I frequented them, and this blind obedience was for me the only path I could follow and my very last hope of survival (D. 77).

When for the first time this moment was drawing near, I was snatched from it by virtue of holy obedience (D. 99).

This virtue has such an immense value because it is the greatest virtue of Christ in His redemptive work after Love.¹⁴⁰ Jesus explained this to His beloved daughter:

> **I have come to do My Father's will. I obeyed my parents, I obeyed My tormentors and now I obey the priests** (D. 535).

And the Saint responded:

> I understand, O Jesus, the spirit of obedience and in what it consists. It includes not only external performance, but also the reason, the will and judgment. Obeying our superiors, we obey God. It makes no difference whether it is an angel or a man who, acting in God's stead, gives me orders; I must always obey (D. 535).

Such acts are not irrational nor involuntary; for religious obedience is understood as "loyal submission of the will and intellect"¹⁴¹, and thus surpasses nature and becomes part of the "logic of grace", "the obedience of faith for the sake of His name" (*Rom* 1:5; cf. 16:26). It means: God has the last word! Saint Padre Pio put it once in this way: "The authority can err, obedience never."¹⁴²

St. Faustina's inspirations were clear: God asks obedience towards His representatives, in the *formum internum* or towards the confessor, and in the *forum externum* or towards the legitimate superiors:

---

[140] Cf. *Phil* 2:6-8; *Heb* 5:8-9; 10:7; *Jn* 4:34.

[141] Vatican II, *Lumen Gentium*, 25.

[142] In Marco TOSATTI, *Padre Pio e il Diavolo*, 50.

Jesus ... said, ... **Be absolutely as frank as possible with your confessor** (D. 1499; cf. D. 1760).

And, with regard to the exterior authority, she was given the following advice:

> When I told Father, he was quite different and he said to me, "sister, don't be afraid of anything. ... If you are obedient and persevere in this disposition, you need not worry about anything. God will find a way to bring about His work. You should always have this simplicity and sincerity and tell everything to Mother General. What I said to you was said as a warning, because illusions may afflict even holy persons, and Satan's insinuations may play a part in this, and sometimes this comes from our own selves, so one has to be careful. And so continue as you have thus far ..." (D. 646).

Saint Faustina, who suffered especially from the request of Jesus to found a new Congregation, never had the courage to act or do anything by herself. She was aware that:

> ... a person will not go far by himself, and Satan wants just this: to have the person who is aspiring for sanctity direct himself because then, without doubt, he will never attain it (D. 938).

A soul that will not fully submit its inspirations to the strict control of the Church; that is, to the director, clearly shows by this that a bad spirit is guiding it. The director should be extremely prudent in such cases and test the soul's obedience. Satan can even clothe himself in a cloak of humility, but he does not know how to wear the cloak of obedience and thus his evil designs will be disclosed (D. 939).

This reveals that the enemy also has weak points. He is not like God, the absolute Truth and Good. He might be able to deceive for a time, but, in his root, he is basically always *proud*. He thinks that he is greater than he is, and therefore is a *liar* (enemy of the truth) and *disobedient* (enemy of the good). This does not mean to deny the value of the virtue of humility in the quoted text, but Faustina learnt: "Satan defeats only the proud and the cowardly" (D. 450).

6.4.8 ACTIVE VIGILANCE

These observations of the spiritual life of Saint Faustina show how important serene, constant and active vigilance is. This comes forth from the love of God, of oneself and of our neighbor. Love is the greatest help and defense against temptations; it is the fruit of grace which leads to continuous work and the conscious fulfillment of personal obligations.

It is the responsibility of not only confessors, spiritual directors, Superiors, and all directors of souls to be vigilant; also it is the first duty for every individual soul in particular[143].

---

[143] Saint Faustina confesses that one helps the other: "From the moment He gave me a spiritual director, I have been more faithful to grace. Thanks to the director and his watchfulness over my soul, I have learned what guidance means and how

The help of spiritual direction brings security to souls in their walk through unknown areas, but it does not free them from striving for perfection.

> When, under his direction, my soul began to experience deep recollection and peace, I often heard these words in my soul: **Strengthen yourself for combat** - repeated over and over at various times (D. 145).

This was the warning Jesus gave repeatedly before He went back to the Father: "Watch!" (Mt 24:42; cf. 25:12-13); watch and be prepared (cf. Mt 24:43): "Watch and pray that you may not enter into temptation; the spirit indeed is willing, but the flesh is weak" (Mt 26:41).

Saint Faustina confesses:

> Despite the peace in my soul, I fight a continuous battle with the enemy of my soul. More and more, I am discovering his traps, and the battle flares up anew (D. 1287).

> My Jesus, despite these graces which You send upon me, I feel that my nature, ennobled though it be, is not completely stilled; and so I keep a constant watch. I must struggle with many faults, knowing well that it is not the struggle which debases one, but cowardice and failure (D. 1340).

Jesus looks at it. Jesus warned me of the least fault and stressed that He Himself judges the matter that I present to my confessor; and [He told me] that... **any transgressions against the confessor touch Me Myself "** (D. 145).

Another time, she confesses the need of constant vigilance.

> My Jesus, despite Your graces, I see and feel all my misery. I begin my day with battle and end it with battle. As soon as I conquer one obstacle, ten more appear to take its place. But I am not worried, because I know that this is the time of struggle, not peace (D. 606).

We recall the words of Jesus: "Do you think that I have come to give peace on earth? No, I tell you, but rather division" (*Lk* 12:51)! And another: "From the days of John the Baptist until now the kingdom of heaven has suffered violence, and men of violence take it by force" (*Mt* 11:12-13). However, Saint Faustina made it clear that this constant attentiveness was not a threat that made her nervous. Confidence overcomes all fear; the surrender to God gives strength:

> When the burden of the battle becomes too much for me, I throw myself like a child into the arms of the heavenly Father and trust I will not perish. O my Jesus, how prone I am to evil, and this forces me to be constantly vigilant. But I do not lose heart. I trust God's grace, which abounds in the worst misery (D. 606; cf. D. 1630).

Her inner peace even turns out to be a weapon that weakens her enemies.

> In the midst of the worst difficulties and adversities, I do not lose inner peace or exterior balance, and this discourages my adversaries.

Patience in adversity gives power to the soul (D. 607).

Her Guardian Angel gave Saint Faustina these encouraging words: "Do not fear, spouse of my Lord; without His permission these spirits will do you no harm" (D. 419), and her Divine spouse adds: "**Your vigilance pleases Me**" (D. 1787).

The Angels do not wish us to be afraid, anxious, and nervous. Rather, they want us to have interior peace while we fight our spiritual battles here on earth, until one day, we will sing the mercies of our Lord together with the Choirs of Angels and Saints in the Glory of heaven.

"In the presence of the Angels I will sing your praises, oh Lord!" (*Ps* 138:1).

CONCLUSION

THE ANGELOLOGY IN THE DIARY OF SAINT FAUSTINA

The study of the *Diary* of Saint Faustina gives an opportunity to look into the world of the Angels and to their presence in man's life. After having explored such richness in these notes, it seems appropriate to try to summarize Saint Faustina's contribution to an Angelology. The principle points of such a summary would be these:

The Angels in themselves:

The Angels

- are creatures;
- don't comprehend God fully, still less His mercy;
- are individuals and persons like Saint Michael, Angels of sacred places and Guardian Angels;
- are divided into nine choirs;
- posses distinct characteristics as beauty, luminosity, intelligence, love;
- passed a test in which some failed;
- who separated from God now persecute men with great hatred.

The Angels in the "Communion of Saints"

The Angels

- adore, praise and give thanks to God Father, Son and Holy Spirit (with all the Saints);
- defend the justice of God before creatures;
- incline themselves before the love and Mercy of God towards men;
- serve the sanctification and salvation of men;
- are sent also from the highest choirs (e.g. the Seraph to bring holy Communion; the Cherub to protect a gate);
- dedicate themselves to greater and lower services (e.g. company on trips);
- protect and defend men before the fallen angels;
- cooperate with men for the good of the souls (e.g. inspiring prayers for the dying).

Human beings are not alone in this world! God, His grace, and love never fail. Pope Francis expresses it in this message:

St Michael the Archangel, Patron of the Vatican City State ... is the champion of the primacy of God, of his transcendence and power.

Michael fights to reestablish divine justice; he defends the people of God from their enemies and above all from the arch-enemy par excellence, the devil.

And St Michael triumphs because in him it is God who acts.

This sculpture reminds us therefore that evil is vanquished, the accuser is unmasked, his head is crushed, because salvation was fulfilled once and for all by the blood of Christ.

Even if the devil is always trying to scratch the face of the Archangel and the face of man, God is stronger; his is the victory and his salvation is offered to every human being.

On the journey and in the trials of life we are not alone, we are accompanied and sustained by the Angels of God, who offer, so to speak, their wings to help us overcome the many dangers, to be able to fly above those realities that can make our lives difficult or drag us down.

In consecrating the Vatican City State to St Michael the Archangel, let us ask him to defend us from the Evil One and cast him out.[144]

Angels and Saints, brothers and sisters unite themselves with all human beings by divine Providence. Everyone needs to rely on these

---

[144] *L'Osservatore Romano*, weekly engl. edition, July 10, 2013, page 7.

heavenly companions, the Holy Angels! Human beings cannot forget about them!

> I thanked God for His goodness, that He gives us angels for companions. Oh, how little people reflect on the fact that they always have beside them such a guest, and at the same time a witness to everything! Remember, sinners, that you likewise have a witness to all your deeds (D. 630).

Let us unite with the prayer of Saint Faustina:

> Jesus, my spirit yearns for You, and I desire very much to be united with You, but Your works hold me back. ... Let everything You have planned before the ages be fulfilled in me, O my Creator and Lord! It is only Your word that I understand; it alone gives me strength. Your Spirit, O Lord, is the Spirit of Peace; and nothing troubles my depths because You dwell there, O Lord.

> I know that I am under Your special gaze, O Lord. ... I do not fear anything, although the storm is raging, and frightful bolts strike all around me, and I then feel quite alone. Yet, my heart senses You, and my trust grows, and I see all Your omnipotence which upholds me. With You, Jesus, I go through life, amid storms and rainbows, with a cry of joy, singing the song of Your mercy. I will not stop singing my song of love until the choir of Angels picks it up. There is no power that can stop me in my flight toward God (D. 761).

The presence of the holy Angels in the life of man explains the prayer of the Church:

> GOD our Father, in Your loving providence You send Your holy Angels to watch over us. Hear our prayers, defend us always by their protection and let us share Your life with them for ever.[145]

With the help of the holy Angels one can be sure: "In spite of Satan's anger, the Divine Mercy will triumph over the whole world and will be worshipped by all souls" (D. 1789).

---

[145] *Liturgy of the Hours*, Evening prayer on October 2, Memorial of the Guardian Angels.

NUMBERS QUOTED FROM THE DIARY

For the holy Angels:

17, 20, 30, 69, 80, 85, 98, 116, 159, 161, 180, 195, 220, 238, 240, 278, 309, 314, 319, 334, 361, 367, 394, 412, 418, 419, 470, 471, 474, 475, 480, 490, 492, 522, 534, 535, 566, 630, 635, 637, 651, 667, 683, 699, 706, 741, 761, 779, 781, 819, 820, 824, 825, 828, 834, 835, 873, 949, 995, 1022, 1049, 1061, 1111, 1126, 1135, 1172, 1174, 1200, 1202, 1215, 1220, 1231, 1240, 1271, 1278, 1324, 1332, 1339, 1350, 1369, 1393, 1427, 1489, 1553, 1556, 1565, 1584, 1604, 1605, 1632, 1676, 1677, 1680, 1692, 1718, 1722, 1735, 1741, 1742, 1743, 1745, 1746, 1791, 1799, 1804, 1805, 1808, 1810, 1821.

For the fallen angels:

40, 48, 76, 79, 96, 97, 99, 129, 130, 145, 159, 173, 240, 300, 307, 311, 320, 323, 356, 378, 411, 412, 418, 419, 420, 429, 450, 480, 496, 520, 540, 601, 633, 643, 644, 646, 666, 673, 674, 686, 713, 723, 741, 745, 764, 812, 858, 873, 938, 939, 949, 1052, 1086, 1115, 1127, 1167, 1287, 1338, 1339, 1340, 1384, 1405, 1411, 1465, 1479, 1485, 1488, 1489, 1496, 1497, 1498, 1499, 1535, 1558, 1560, 1565, 1570, 1580, 1583, 1646, 1659, 1715, 1720, 1742, 1743, 1760, 1768, 1789, 1791, 1798, 1799, 1802.

Are you called to become a Canon Regular of the Holy Cross?

The Order of Canons Regular of the Holy Cross is a religious community of pontifical rite. It was founded in Coimbra, Portugal in the year 1131. St. Theotonius was the first Prior of the Order. With permission of Pope St. John Paul II, the Order was restored in 1979. It is now present in 11 countries.

In union with the holy Angels, to whom the entire Order and each individual member are consecrated, and after the model of the Apostles, the Order celebrates the sacred Liturgy as the center of its life.

In communion with the Angels and Saints, the members of Order cultivate a special veneration to the Passion of Our Lord and strive after a perfect conformity to the love of our Crucified Lord.

One of the apostolates of the Order is to preach retreats and promote a devotion to the holy Angels as a special need for our times, incorporating the help of the holy Angels in the spiritual conflicts that are present in the Church and the world. The Holy See has given the Order governance of the *Work of the Holy Angels*.

With the holy Angels as fellow servants, the Order regards as its foremost tasks: serving the sanctification of the priestly state, offering expiation for priests, assisting struggling priests and strengthening the faith in the priesthood among the lay-faithful.

The Sisters of the Holy Cross form with the Order and the *Work of the Holy Angels* one spiritual family.

If you are interested in more information, visit our web sites: www.cruzios.org; www.opusangelorum.org

The author: Fr. Titus Kieninger, is a member of the Order of Canons Regular of the Holy Cross. He was ordained to the priesthood in 1977. He serves as professor of philosophy and theology in the Institutum Sapientiae in the diocese of Anápolis, Brazil (http://institutumsapientiae.org). He also preaches retreats and offers spiritual direction. He has published other works on the angels. In English, there is the book: Discernment of Spirits in our Times.